NORTH EAST INDIA
GLOBALIZATION AND SARVODAYA

About the Author

J.N. Nanda, with a string of academic distinctions including two earned doctorates, multitude of awards from the IBC and American Biography Association, and other national and international awards, is a distinguished scientist, thinker and writer. Prof. Nanda attended on Invitation in USA, the International Conference on the Unity of Sciences. He has led Indian delegations to Australia, UK, and had invitation visits to Prague, Washington DC, Tokyo and London. He has been the founder president of the Secular Life Society of India. He has summarized his all embracing philosophy and religion as New Mahayana in which all 'isms' co-exist. Among his scientific contributions, mention can be made of his new light on the earth's internal structure, the origin of the moon and the origin of earth's magnetism etc. He has travelled practically in all continents and studied many languages. Besides his scientific books and publications, mention may be made of his book *"Science and Technology in India's Transformation"*, released by the President of India at the Rashtrapati Bhawan in 1986. Other important books are *Foreign Policy of Co-existence—India, Glimpses of Indian History and Culture,* and *Co-operative Development of Marine Resources, Religion and Philosophy for Modern Youth, Bengal, the Unique State, Human Eternity: Stone Age to Mustopia.*

North East India Globalization and Sarvodaya

J.N. Nanda

CONCEPT PUBLISHING COMPANY, NEW DELHI-110 059

Cataloging in Publication Data—DK
Courtesy: D.K. Agencies (P) Ltd. <docinfo@dkagencies.com>

Nanda, J. N. (Jatinder Nath), 1920-
North East India : globalization and Sarvodaya / J.N. Nanda.
p. cm.
Includes bibliographical references (p.)
Includes index.
ISBN 13: 9788180695018
ISBN 10: 8180695018

1. Globalization—Social aspects—India, Northeastern. 2. India, Northeastern—Social conditions. 3. Sarvodaya movement—India, Northeastern. I. Title.

DDC 301.095 41 22

ISBN-13: 978-81-8069-501-8
ISBN-10: 81-8069-501-8

First Published 2008

Published and Printed by
Ashok Kumar Mittal
Concept Publishing Company
A/15-16, Commercial Block, Mohan Garden
New Delhi-110059 (INDIA)

Phones : 25351460, 25351794
Fax : 091-11-25357103
Email : publishing@conceptpub.com

Foreword

The North Eastern region of India (NEI) is an integral part of the Union and has a great significance politically, strategically, economically and culturally. Its high profile in regional cultures, ethnicity, history and languages fits very well in India known for its mosaic of diverse elements in all these aspects. Since independence and the adoption of our Constitution, our emphasis is on unity in diversity. Howsoever different our institutions, social ways, culinary and sartorial practices may be, there is a common thread of patriotism and a deep feeling of sharing a common destiny marking our existence during the last six decades. The northern part of India is known for its Aryan ethos, the southern peninsula is recognized for its ancient Dravid past, the NEI represents Mongoloid India with distinctive ethno-cultural features. Geographically it is bounded by Myanmar, Bangladesh, Bhutan, Tibet and Nepal. The region is inhabited by many tribes speaking a large number of languages quite distinct from one another.

It is a quirk of destiny that in this region, the people so vigorous and dynamic, instead of channelising their energies and resources for forging ahead in every field, began succumbing to jealousies, dissensions and digressions. The youth in motivation for quick political gains spear-headed the many separatist movements. It is more probable that some political forces on the borders of India sowed the seeds of disharmony as a part of their long range expectation of disintegration of the Indian Union. It cannot be dismissed out of hand that India has been rankling in the minds of some powerful nations who were never able to reconcile themselves to seeing India emerge as one of the strong poles in the present day multi-polar world after having remained a big colony of a small imperialist nation from afar. The

outsiders have been nudging the sons of the soil towards dissent and dissipation, conflict, turmoil and confrontation.

The author of this slender volume, Prof. J.N. Nanda, a Geo-physicist by training and a defence scientist by profession has been exploring the avenues of history, religion, secularism and spiritualism for many years. Lately he has spent considerable time in the study of the NEI situation and its environment for identifying the roots of disaffection of the disgruntled elements in the region which has become a cause of anxiety to the country and has provided grist to the mill of speculation about the boastful unity of the country and the lasting cohesion of the structure of the Indian civilization. Prof. Nanda, apparently is an uncompromising optimist with firm faith in the eternal continuity of India as a strong pillar of strength and fountain of energy. In his firm belief he gives a few billion years for the planet earth to survive and with it the unity of India in the world's march to progress.

Along with above, he predicts a worldwide silent revolution towards an inevitable utopia for whole mankind that he calls *"Mustopia"*. He feels that an era is not far off when entire humanity including all Indians will be subscribing to this new belief advocating peace, justice and fairplay for all, banishing malpractices, self-aggrandizement, violence and exploitation. In the fair deal for our people in the NEI, there will be some generosity to them in the simultaneous efforts to bring them into the national mainstream. Many years have been lost in the indifferent handling of the affairs of this most colourful and volatile region of India. Sarvodaya is the panacea for resolving the grievances: real or imaginary, of that part of India. The author pleads for all sided progress and development of the NEI, giving fillip to the local autonomy, preservation of their cultural ethos and providing the tribal people an honourable place in the Indian family and on the world stage, a place of dignity and grace.

The present volume makes an interesting reading though everyone may not share his particular expectation of *Mustopia* on the horizon in few centuries.

Manohar Singh Batra

New Delhi *Former Director General, All India Radio*

Preface and Acknowledgements

This book deals with the possible stance of the North East India (NEI) in future that can bring credit to the nation as a model multi-ethnic state. Indian philosophy from ancient times has sought unity in diversity. India has a past of uniform progress from tribal origins. The additional element was placing trust on logic and reason that combined humanism and secularism with religious belief in love and empathy for others. It was the Indian genius that spread Buddhist Mahayana that brought peace and progress to the known world for many centuries around the birth of Christ.

The author is one among many who realizes that peace and progress are indivisible for the whole humanity. Setting up of UN is a miracle and a sign that it would be fully empowered to assure internal and external stability and security to all nations, big or small. Only now people are realizing that jealous gods are not hurling dooms-day on the world, but humanity will last at least for an eternity (at least couple of billion years more) of the earth. The immense vista of future progress has opened up and need not be wasted in wrong policies of up-man-ship and confrontation. Another miracle happened when Newton laid the foundation of modern science and technology. The human achievements for common good and easing of all kinds of burden in the last couple of centuries have been remarkable. The opportunity exists now of achieving heaven on earth as was the ambition of all great dreamers for few like-minded people. Now it is clear that the expected utopia will arise if it is the common goal of whole humanity. It is *mustopia* for the entire world. We can either traverse the road to *Mustopia*

or perish in internal discord and external confrontations. Progress of ethnic pockets of all nations will be the first fruit of advancing prosperity in peace and fellowship. The present century is crucial for starting on the *Mustopia* course. The UN has to be further strengthened. The UN governance through international collaborations and the tools of national governments will encompass all humanity. NEI is blessed with vigorous young blood and a fertile and rich part of India which is already confirmed as a welfare state. By embracing the Indian concerns for humanism and secularism and philosophical acceptance of *sarvodaya, i.e.* better life for all the NEI will also reach its goals. In chapter seven brief notes are added describing "globalization", "Mustopia", "New Mahayana", "Sarvodaya" and "Secularism" for ready reference.

Acknowledgements

It gives me great pleasure to express my gratitude to my friend Shri Manohar Singh Batra to not only agree to write a foreword to this book but also to go through the entire manuscript.

Contents

1

Introduction

North East India

North East India (NEI) deserves special attention of India of which it is an integral part. Communications within NEI are underdeveloped like those in other neighbouring countries. In earlier times when communications were primitive restricted to traffic on foot or in small boats or on elephants for crossing jungles that abounded in this region, it acted as the hub of the wheel of trade between India and its Bengal plains with countries of the north and east like Tibet, Nepal, Bhutan, China, Myanmar, Malayasia, Java and Thailand. Pre-historic migrations of people occurred along the Brahmaputra valley and the valleys of its tributaries. Some scholars hold that a section of ancient Hindus travelled south along the Brahmaputra from the north. They cite proofs from names of villages and lakes that the Ramayana story actually was enacted in the Brahmaputra valley and point out ancient true sites of Ayodhya, Janak Puri and Sri Lanka (an island in a vast lake formed by the river Brahmaputra).

The seven Indian states that comprise NEI are: Meghalaya, Assam, Arunachal Pradesh, Nagaland, Mizoram Manipur and Tripura. Five of these states were parts of Assam province of British India. About 50 per cent of the population of NEI is tribal. The tribes constitute in their reckoning many independent tribal "nations" jealous of their traditional culture and autonomy. A central tribal authority

was never in the reckoning. In the 14th century, the Ahoms who had carved a home in Myanmar on migration from Thailand, stormed into NEI and occupied Assam which they ruled as Hindus for next six centuries, defending the integrity of their empire from in-roads of both Pathans and Moguls and later from the tentacles of the British East India Company entrenched in Bengal. In the 18th century, the proud king of Myanmar laid claim to be the overlord of Assam and his forces laid waste the peaceful kingdom of Ahoms. The British would not relish having a strong Myanmar on the doorstep of their possessions in India. The defeat of the Burmese king by the British company's forces led to the annexation of Assam to the Indian empire of the British, but the British did not relish direct control over the ever feuding tribes and decided to perpetuate the tribal authorities of various clans and to exercise indirect control over the area. They reasoned from anthropological basics to allow natural evolution of the tribes and desired to leave them alone so long as they were not disturbing the life of peaceful plains people in Bengal. In place of growth of traditional culture, the central indifference led to the expected decay in the tribal life and loss in the natural quality of the tribal people. The only civilizing influence allowed to function by the British and then by scholarly Nehru was the activities of various Christian missions and later by the Hindu missionary societies. The new features introduced by these were the wide adoption of the Roman alphabet and the introduction of English as a language among the native dialects of the NEI. Since the Christian Karen's opposition to the independence of Myanmar, the Indian political parties were not friendly to the conversion of the tribals to Christianity.

In the struggle for Indian independence, many Assamese and Manipuris as well as others participated and were active in the deliberations of the Constituent Assembly that architectured the new government of free India with

assurance of autonomy to minorities, minority languages and minority religions. India was reorganizsed into autonomous linguistic states of the future with special consideration of underdeveloped hill states.

End of British Rule in 1947

The British quit India in 1947. The tribal leaders also dreamt of riddance from any central authority and of curbs on their exploitation of the superstitious tribal population. The Nagas were in the forefront of the rebellions for independence. The Indian authorities had a serious problem of controlling the Naga movement. It has not completely died yet and it gave rise to many parallel movements for independence of other groups notably Mizos and some factions of Nagas in other states of the North East. The Bodos of north hills region of Assam are the latest to join the clamour for an autonomous district. The rebel bands when chased, often found sanctuary in Bangladesh which had won freedom from Pakistan with the moral and material support of India, but had entrenched in its governing strata pro-Pakistan elements which still held on to the policy discarded even by the people of present Pakistan, that of India baiting. Bangladesh was also afraid that India will try to throw out illegal Bangladeshi settlers from NEI including Hindu-Buddhist Chakmas that had been expelled from East Pakistan (or Bangladesh) through communal atrocities on non-Muslims there. Mizo rebels had created their own sanctuaries on Bhutanese soil. In support of Indian policy, the Bhutanese eventually destroyed these sanctuaries and the Mizos seem to have settled in peace in their autonomous full-fledged Mizoram state. All the while the government of India has tried to make progress in the development efforts. Many new institutes that provide know-how and training of various kinds have been set up. The NEI is covered by forests and homesteads. The inefficient Jhum cultivation is giving way to settled

agriculture, but there is acute land hunger and it is difficult even to meet essential land requirements for institutional development or for development of agricultural extension and for popularizing new agricultural methods.

The current friction between Naga ambition of an extended Nagalim and historical existence of Manipur state with overlordship over its hill Nagas will ease out in view of a united effort for democratic advancement of the entire NEI. The development effort must persist but it should be pursued with consideration of tribal sensitivity. Adequate compensation and consideration should be given to tribal leaders when they show a spirit of cooperation in the coming period of globalization and development over the entire world. The significance of growing pre-eminence of UN governance must not be lost on the local leadership. The states of NEI when they dream of independent nationhood seem to have no concern for feasibility or economic viability. They seem to rely on a wild belief in their violence against unarmed villagers and success in past local strife. For the ethnic militias, the major financing has been from the extortion demands termed taxation by the rebels who claim to run a parallel government in some disturbed areas. Some of these bring to mind the happenings in Angola before it ended its civil wars. For some time insurgency is countered by counter insurgency. This leads to further impoverishment since true advance will only come through more production and better development effort. The sooner better agriculture, forest management and animal husbandry are attempted, the better it will be for the economy of the NEI.

Social pressures have created fake myths of ancient greatness of vanished cities and forgotten grandeur. There is considerable glory in the imagined past from the surmised spread of Hindu-Buddhism across these territories into Myanmar and beyond. All this can lead to considerable lucrative tourism and safaris in the NEI when supported by the required tourism, the infrastructure for which has yet to be in place.

Prologue

NEI started its modern period in 2001 when India set up a ministry at the centre to push the development of NEI. Certain states had been created to meet the demands of the insurgency by acceding to give full state status to Arunachal Pradesh, Mizoram and Nagaland in 1972 and Meghalaya and Manipur got full statehood in 1992. Some autonomous districts were also created and are now functioning. The 21st century is crucial to its advancement and marching with India to a new world of internal and external security assured by the developing UN system of governance of democratic participation of all. This prologue deals with happenings since Indian hegemony began with the British Indian acquisition of Assam after the defeat of the Burmese occupation forces in the NEI and the treaty of Yandabo in 1826.

There was regular trade between Bengal and Khasi hill areas. Later, imported steel replaced the native product. Other trade items were coal and horticultural products. But all trade was in the hands of Bengalis and Manipuris. British occupation of Khasi hills helped trade to grow. The tribal folk bought and sold slaves which was forwned upon by the British. The economic and mineral resources have never been properly assessed so far. The Assamese took to trade and business very late. A section of Bengali midle class shifted to Assam to assist the colonial administration and to carry on their own clerical and professional advancement. Bengali speaking minority in Assam is sizeable (22%). There was unrest when Assamese was made the language of courts and given the status of primary language of Assam. The Assamese and Bengalis are however well integrated. This familiarity with Bengali culture and Bengal administrative skill will stand NEI in good stead in future when cooperation with Bangladesh and impetus to communications with India and Myanmar across Bangladesh will enhance trade, commerce and industrialization of both.

Khasis of Khasi hills could not forge unity. They had numerous chiefs nown as Siems. Assam suffered terrible chaos during Burmese invasion of 1817-1824. The Ahom kingdom got recreated in 1833. Marwaris and Bengali Muslims came as traders or they came to help grow rice on terraces. Settlers among them soon became part of the new middle class. Ethno national upsurges are a challenge to the national state. The world has more than 2000 homeland claims based on ethnicity. Only modernization and development based on equality can satisfy them. Multi-culturalism has to be reinforced. The Soviet experiment of a multi-national state has failed, but this prescription is still voiced by the communists of India. The melting pot theory is also discredited. Distinct cultures do not give up their identity easily. Drastic measures for the submergence of mini cultures or ethnic purification are repugnant to the human sense of fair play. The state must exist to enforce its laws so that the citizens live in harmony. India is pumping in money through the newly set up ministry at Centre for the development of NEI and for counter insurgency. The ULFA fighting for the liberation of Assam is countered by the counter insurgents SULFA from the surrendered rebels. The future lies with strengthening of democracy and regard for human rights of all. Bureaucratic enthusiasm often produced criminalization of the tribes. The government must pursue its policy of finding democratic solutions by discussion. Already demands for homelands for the Mizos and the Nagas have been met. The situation is of increasing demands for homelands by many tribes which would mean break up of NEI into non-viable autonomous units or to the balkanization of NEI. Where possible, district councils with some judicial powers and own police force have been established. Re-organization of Assam in 1972 gave full statehood to Nagaland, Mizoram and Arunachal Pradesh. Meghalaya and Manipur also became separate states. Future now lies with

the Indian and global institutions active in the peace and progress of NEI. We need cohesion of all people in India.

A middle class has emerged in Assam as in other Indian states out of government servants, lawyers and those having rights in land. Assam is the home of Indian silk production and most girls are expert in weaving which they learn at the mothers' knee. Assam has been exporting metal wares, mats, ivory, timber and timber products. Final British imperial battle with the Nagas ended in 1858. The British decided to leave the tribes alone so long as they did not raid civilian targets in Bengal and Assam. A technical institute was established in 1932 in Shillong. Garos had rapid change for the better from taking to plough cultivation, Christian educative intrusion and the development of communications. Communists were active particularly in Tripura where an anti-Bengali agitation erupted. Tribal priests replaced Brahman priests in certain temples. Landlessness and indebtedness arose during the British occupation as in other parts of India. Protective discrimination in favour of tribals has continued. The constituent assembly did not concede the formation of a Khasi state; only in 1972, Khasis became chief constituents of Meghalaya. The tribal districts of north Cachar decided to cast their future with Assam. Bodos demand of a homeland or autonomous district north of the Brahmaputra is pending and so are some other homeland demands. What is urgently desired is scientific management of forests as has been demonstrated under UN auspices in Guatemala of South America. There has been large influx of Biharis and Nepalis causing further shortage of land for the native population especially where Jhum cultivation is still practiced. Several tribes still treat women as a commodity. The education is a big task. Some relief must be found from the existence in NEI of 325 distinct languages and twenty-five scripts. Hindi, Assamese, English and Bengali have a lot of scope to flourish in these areas.

Nagas and Manipur

On India's independence, Nagas and Manipur both were not much interested in merging with India and preferred independent treaty relationships with India. India could not very well agree to this. Nehru was willing to launch armed forces to effect integration of any such areas. Due to playing faction politics India succeeded in providing the boon of affiliation to India, but discontent continued to simmer. The insurgents could get sanctuaries outside the country. India had to weather the harm from insurgency and counter insurgency. The democratic process however continued and Jamir, a Naga leader became the chief minister of Assam. Phizo, the rebel Naga leader who usually stayed abroad finally agreed to give up confrontation if statehood was accorded to Nagaland, the compact Naga area at the border with Myanmar. Manipur had a Hindu faction, but its majority population particularly in the hill tracts to the north was Naga but a different clan from the one in control of Nagaland. When soon the Nagas started an agitation for greater Nagaland at the cost of Manipur, any acceptance by India would be to alienate completely the Manipur state and the Manipur Nagas. Both sides have to be satisfied in mutual interest by living in harmony. It is like the conflict situation in unified state of Bombay combining Maharashtra and Gujarat. India almost forced them to continue to hold together, but to no avail. Soon these had to be separated and there is no longer any animosity between them. This separation already exists between Nagaland and Manipur but both are unhappy with the *status quo.* The Manipuris cite historical conflict free co-existence of Manipur population of all races and creeds. They blame India for speedily agreeing to full state status of Nagaland, which is just a cluster of Nagas of various clans and now they are ambitious to expand their hegemony over other Nagas. The democratic solution would be a popular vote of hill people in Manipur. The best way to get to the desire of the

population would be to hold elections to Manipur Assembly with the revised electoral lists and then allow the representatives from the hill areas to meet separately for a vote for rejoining their colleagues of Manipur or for opting out. In that event the best way would be to give them an autonomous district free from control from Nagaland or from Manipur. There can be common governor for Nagaland and Manipur with special interest in justice to minorities of both states. The suspicions, we are certain, will fade away if administration is on the road to *Mustopia* with goodwill for all. Governance through rebellion and violence is no longer a viable alternative in India wedded to democracy and justice for all. Manipur will be within its rights to accord English the status of preferred language along with Hindi and other languages. The Manipur University may have a separate unit for the hill people of Manipur and admit others who may qualify for entrance including other Nagas in the NEI.

It is quite in the interest of the Manipuris that militancy ends there and the state settles into peaceful mode of reconstruction. The violation of human rights will continue if the state continues to be governed by armed forces special powers as if it is war time. Naga leaders both in Nagaland as well as of the Naga tribes in Manipur should seriously work on the organization of a joint Nagalim-Manipur state as Jammu and Kashmir is constituted. Bodos and Korbis demands of autonomous districts could be extended to other areas, if necessary, of the joint large state. It is too late for a mini constituent assembly for the NEI to focus on all pending aspirations including those of Bodos and Korbis. It should be clarified at start that full-fledged appendage of an assembly, a governor, and ministers will not be possible for every autonomous district. They can only get a single administrator holding an elected office for five years with a budget allotment each year by the state and central governments. The administrator will be head of the district police, district planning board and the administration will be through existing channels keeping the administrator fully

in the picture. The popular government need not be top-heavy. It should be the cheapest form of governance with the cooperation of the public.

Why Develop?

The primitive slash and burn agriculture cannot support even the much lower population than what is now driven to much less land. Even the gathering of jungle produce and catching of fish are insufficient. The tribal people were ever alert against intrusion of outsiders. In Mizoram there was violent expulsion of outsiders and refugees from Myanmar. There arose practically mob rule everywhere and the administration never reached the hills and valleys of NEI away from large towns. The government and police were enmeshed in insurgency and counter-insurgency. The government of India accepted the policy of positive discrimination in favour of the local people and residents who were recent immigrants and not second generation immigrants without voting rights could in principle be deported. The refugees and permitted immigrant workers could corner all available land by benami transactions. Even land essential for communication and education infra-structure was scarce. The population had increased four-fold in the first 50 years after independence. Trade, commerce, the engines of prosperity of this area were now languishing on acount of unsettled conditions and lack of entrepreneurial skills. In the climate of might is right, the primitive tribal democracy was crumbling along with tribal organization of the Nagas. There was non-traditional exploitation by the elected officials. The tribal strife came in the way of democratic representation on the autonomous district councils. The Naga National Council, United Liberation Front of Assam (ULFA), the Tripura Upjati Samiti only looked to the privileges of specific groups or clans. Only the government claimed to protect the human rights of all, but its writ was severely eroded by insurgency. Still there

was hope for genuine service. The tribes had responded well to the spirit of service shown by Christian and Hindu missionaries. There was hope that outsiders can again be welcome if they come on invitation as agents of change and assist in training and development as per requirement of the local authorities. The experts believe that the NEI with its unutilized resources of raw materials, waste lands periodically inundated by flood waters, thick forests and scenic beauty when properly developed and supported by tourism infrastructure can easily bring about prosperity to the entire population. They must start with a will on the development course involving setting up of agricultural, animal husbandry, forestry and engineering workshops. Education has to spread and the gains in popularizing the Roman alphabet and common use of English as the vehicle for higher learning have to be expanded. Linguistic chauvinism should be replaced by pragmatic policies of hard work and diligent apprenticeship of every kind that can promote entrepreneurship and setting up of secondary repair shops and first processing of agricultural and forest produce. There is great potential of export of fruit and flowers, timber and timber or cane products. The NEI can develop and export hydroelectric power and even ask for a contribution from plains people who use the water flowing out of NEI, but the NEI should also have expertise of flood control that damage the land in the plains.

Khasi alphabet was developed by the missionaries and first Khasi press started in 1896. Assamese language is rich in literature. Manipur has contributed to eastern literature profusely. The NEI has only to shake away failed dogmas of development and take to the time tested path of service and cooperation to get out of the pond of despair and dependence. They have all the ingredients for development.

Historically NEI was ravaged in 1817-1824 by the invasion of the Myanmar king. The primitive society had hardly recovered when the comparative isolation was shattered by the influx of refugees due to partition of India

and then was bedeviled by the insurgency and counter insurgency. The insurgency was only for the right of the ethnic population. Now the whole world and particularly India is for their rights and even positive discrimination in their favour. A number of autonomous states and district councils have been set up meeting most of the wishes of the tribals insurgency. All realistic advances in political organization which do not impinge on the democratic rights of others have an element of possibility now without hindering the march to progress and globalization of trade, commerce and investments as well as expansion of training avenues.

Development of NEI

The pseudo intellectual leaders suspect all development projects as snares to divert people from the true struggle in class war against feudal and exploiting capitalists. They believe in heating up the revolutionary struggle and anarchy so long as their leadership at the end is assured. A developed and peaceful countryside would mean an end to their fishing in troubled waters. Tribals anarchy suited them and the traditional leadership. The entrepreneurship class is blissfully missing and so are the trained manpower to man even the minor technical or administrative positions. The state and central governments as well as the emerging educated and budding capitalists from among retiring officials would like to forge ahead with development projects utilizing controlled temporary import of workers and technical and administrative personnel from neighbouring states. Already the British have demonstrated the success of tea plantations in Assam by such means. But the critics point to the exploitative nature of imported workers who have not made the tea industry really an Assam industry. Only now with the imported Indian capital and expertise some progress is being made in indigenizing the tea production and marketing. Assam has been rich in mineral resources and the proper pace of development has never

been attempted. First there was the imperial interest of British entrepreneurs and later the continuation of anarchic uprisings thwarted the development efforts. The real shortcoming in educational and technical competence will have to be rectified by a concerted programme of providing technical institutions for all levels of workers. The NEI in vast spaces is like the darkest of dark Africa. Slowly the tribal diffidence from using helping hands from their educated compatriots will ease and development projects and necessary institutes for education and training will be allowed to come up. The central government is evidently willing to make the seed financial investments. Tax income is necessary but "taxes" collected by rebels go into counter development. Peace is a necessary condition for lasting development efforts. The creative talents of the population as are obvious in their artistic creation in straw and weaves have to be harnessed to increase trade and commerce which are the sinews of progress. The globalization is bound to increase tourism and any expansion of infrastructure to help tourism will help NEI. The limited bus and train communications can also serve for tourist stay for a day or so at the terminal stations in the absence of hotels and city market places. Traffic junctions can also create temporary local production emporia for the visitors. It was most interesting to see the entire railway staff both on the train or on the stations on the way, pitching in as salesmen.

Plus Points

The NEI has many plus points for its future prosperity. It exists on the periphery of India, a nation committed to peace and friendship with other countries. India believes in the development of the entire nation including the lowliest in income and education. India is continuously improving its laws and court procedures in favour of removing bottlenecks created by vested interests in the development work. India is against any doctrinaire opposition to creation of wealth

and entrepreneurial activity in the expansion of production. It believes in the fact that when the poor grow richer, the wealthy also benefit. During the period of British rule, the Indians were naturally suspicious of the British development efforts which however were sometimes quite sincere based on the efforts of well meaning British educated civil servants. The inertia of suspicion should give way to welcome of developmnt efforts on merits since the basic philosophy is of total development and not development in the interest of any vested interests. There is the accepted goal of *Sarvodaya* or progress of all as enjoined by Mahatma Gandhi. India is a firm supporter of UN governance efforts. The NEI could welcome re-building of communications with neighbours. The NEI needs enormous wealth and international cooperation to control flood devastation each year and to preserve its forest wealth with proper management. The people of NEI have only to affirm their belief in themselves, shed suspicion of "foreign settlers" who have made NEI their home of second generation. The Indians or Bangladeshis should be welcomed for their past and future contribution to their own and NEI prosperity for all its residents.

Globalization

Globalization of trade and commerce has reached the institutional stage. And the people are taking to it because of convenience and personal gain. It is spreading due to increasing individual consciousness of the global situation due to media coverage and easy communication. Globalization is not global sameness but through promotion of local heterogeniety, peace and co-operation, easy transfer of skills and investment funds. Global taste is developing for variety in cuisine. Urban middle class is increasing and cheers for globalization. UN governance is taking on more tasks and is attempting to take on guarantees for internal and external security of nations through worldwide interest in peace, and cooperation for world development and for

making the nature's experiment of mankind a success for the eternity of earth's existence. Policies of coexistence and tolerance, democratic discussion route to solution of problems are in evidence. The global culture is not conflictual but invites people to freely enjoy their culture or mixture of cultures. Such developments are in tune with the complexity of human mind and agreement on millions of years being available for continued progress or for decline through defective thinking for limited selfish objectives. Globalization and transnational manufacture spreads vocational training, creates more jobs. It spreads small ancillary businesses and workshops and education. There is increasing coinage of international parables, proverbs, songs and short stories. The vision of worldwide peace and progress is now glowing bright and beckoning the whole world to develop together.

2

Society and Development

Present Position

The NEI is a geographically isolated corner of India close to international borders. Each state has small development potential on account of small size, and lack of trained man power. There is shortage of land for archaic method of cultivation and lack of proper upkeep of forests and continued unrest about sharing of wealth which is there. The blind rejection of immigrants should cease and controlled immigration of trained labour as well as technicians allowed to promote setting up of minor enterprises in the first instance. The business acumen and production of handicrafts as well as fruit and flowers can be the initial core of trade and commerce. Branches of National laboratories and national industry can be set up with some key staff on loan who will train skeleton staff for future working. All high school graduates should be recruited for four years training stipend in the NEI, in India or other countries with a contract for working for the NEI on return. All developing countries employ this procedure. The economic backwardness is reflected in lower percentage of urban population. The hard working settlers from Bangladesh and Nepal have already proved their worth in tea and rice cultivation. They have also exercised thrift and even when debarred from purchase of land from the tribals, have invested for processing industries and small

businesses. A new class of entrepreneurs is emerging from retired officials and elected councillors. It should be encouraged to multiply and create savings for more investments. Bank loans should be available for enterprising and hard working individuals as is now being done by the rural banks in India. Consolidation of land holdings for cooperative and cluster development can be encouraged by government assisted expansion of the cooperative movement. The states can consider the ethno-centred political structure while development and progress requires creation of wealth, more savings and investments. The invited immigrants do well themselves and also help train others.

There is urgent need for regional development effort including growth of communications and tourism infrastructure, pursuit of health and environmental goals and of flood control. Advanced agriculture methods that improve soil and help in soil conservation are to be employed. India has enough agricultural expertise and could easily open extension stations in each district which will go a long way in spreading the gospel of modernization. An advance has occurred that technical education is using Hindi or English medium and not getting bogged down in discovering new vocabulary in each dialect or local language. Only in Assam and Manipur the local languages are well advanced to become vehicles for information for development.

Social Life

Indian states have a particularly enlightened approach to the rehabilitation and re-employment of erstwhile rebels. Only feudal subordination has to be discontinued and respect for human rights and democratic equality is to be propagated. There has been rapid change in the social life of the tribal society. The dormitory system for adolescent boys is practically extinct. Education for making the folk better tribe or clan members or better nationals of the state

or of the nation is not yet in position. The Gandhi Peace Foundation in Nagaland, and activity of Ramakrishna Mission as well as of the Christian missions are well appreciated. There is ample reason to set up NEI sports authority and a sports complex with vigorous sports and recreation programmes. There could be many more exchange programmes of dance, drama and rituals with other states of India and neighbouring countries. Locally controlled high frequency radio communication transmitting for a small areas should be multiplied as a major educational and levelling apparatus. Mahatma Gandhi stressed the importance of constructive work by youth for their own training and evolution and for action as change agents. This is necessary all over India but particularly in the NEI which has to make up for many lost decades wasted in neglect or self-glorification or in self pity. A national service scheme should be vigorously pursued for the NEI youth as well as the children. Social work should be introduced in schools by starting high school chapters of an organization like the Rotarians. Economic stagnation and exploitation can end only with the growth of democracy. Industrial belts can be constructed in Manipur and Khasi and Jaintia districts.

Manipur suffers from very high level of corruption. The popularity of Marxism-Leninism is only because that bodes ill for Indian main political parties when Indian control seems to them an extension of colonialism. The Indian authorities have to show and develop sympathy for ethnic nationalism that favours the development and peaceful cooperative enterprise.

Education and Training

Education and learning of various skills are the pre-eminent requirement of the NEI. Literacy and primary education is the birthright of every child. A skill in weaving or artistic use of ordinary materials should be part of primary education at home. From early schooling all efforts are to be

made to excite curiosity in the child about his/her surroundings and to raise questions that prompt lessons in science and technology. The schools and clusters of villages have to be furnished with libraries, supply of textbooks and educational equipment including radio receivers, television sets and computers. Such facilities are missing even in advanced states of India. It is our belief that even at some sacrifice, India would be happy to provide a skeleton service in this regard at certain selected sites and then local enterprise must duplicate the educational facility at many other places. Khasi and Garo languages already have elementary science books for schools. The science education at diploma or university level is restricted to books in English and some selected journals and review journals in English. The fluency in English should be widely tutored as in the rest of the country. The Roman alphabet is recognized by most of NEI. The future may bring about the use of Roman alphabet for practically all Indian languages. This can reduce the burden of translating scientific vocabulary in local languages, since the original words can stand as in English. The diploma level scientific education can be eased by this device. Class notes can be prepared by assistance of the teacher and some good students in the class and then mimeographed in the form of textbooks for other students. Meghalaya has made science compulsory in the final school year from 1983. The education will do away with pass/fail examination system. Every course must end in "pass" but take longer or shorter time depending on the grasp and application of the teacher and the students. There should be course credit system so that the course credit can be carried on paper as well as in one's head by the student. The period for all levels of scholastic achievement should be flexible.

Industrialization is a part of many sided progress. The weaver and wicker-work from Assam and NEI are now world famous. The women of NEI excel in spinning and weaving. What may be added is computer assisted supplies and marketing. The business acumen of the organizers of

the milk revolution in Gujarat and elsewhere may be learnt. Due to fragile eco system in certain areas, only sustainable development has to be sought. Handicrafts and small scale industries have to be encouraged. These provide employment whole time or part time to more youth which is also a core aim of development. Total analysis, *i.e.* cultural validity for the project along with routine system analysis should be carried out before the techno-economic survey for the project. Pre-production raw material processing and post-production applications of the product must be thoroughly ascertained so that production can face competition and has a long life. Repair and maintenance services should be located at many places since, these will come under small scale enterprises and can be easily supported financially to create self-employment.

A gold mine has been provided by nature in the scenic and idyllic beauty. It should be clamouring for attention by tourism industry of the country. Tourism can be encouraged deliberately by the government and community effort. Tourists and temporary visitors come to take part in the education and training in agricultural, health or managerial projects should be welcome, but their immigration has to be strictly controlled. Assam is still suffering from continuous trickle of Bangladeshi immigrants. The Assam farmers often become destitute when they are parted from their land ownership through dire necessity. The influx of Hindu refugees from Bangladesh added to Assam problems. The population of NEI went up four times from 1931 to 1971.

Democracy

Already Tripura and Assam have lost native majorities. This also leads to cultural crisis. The new arrivals when they are Bengali speaking should be utilized for educational development of the entire NEI by giving preference in education and IT industries. One can recall how the British ran most of the administration of entire Indian empire by

using the talents of their Bengali babus. Rights of indigenous people to their pre-eminent position in government jobs and contacts should be assured in the business documents. This has already been achieved in Malaysia and many other countries having the same problem. Democracy with assured human rights of all residents will surely ease the situation. A secular approach regarding language and religion has to be impressed in education for peace and progress.

The NEI has genuine complaint that the British found investment capital for tea plantations, timber, oil and associated transportation needs, but the investments have levelled off and not advanced for progress of the NEI. Only recently the NEI Ministry at Delhi has assured some planned investments in these areas. When the raw materials including timber and crude start producing income to the government or the private developers, a fair share should revert to districts of origin in NEI. The Assam movement for the rights of the Assamese was declared a secessionist movement by the leftists of India. Nagas and Mizos also raised slogans of independence. They are now convinced of just treatment in India after their areas have been converted to (autonomous) states of India and some vociferous elements in a compact area assured of district councils. The Assamese society has continued in its peasant-middle class base. In free India and Bangladesh, Assamese and Bengali speaking people will both develop and achieve economic prosperity which is more important than communal saber rattling. Bangladesh will also be weaned away from entrenched *Jehadist* elements. This is also going to happen because of the growing sense of prosperity through peace and progress, through cooperation of all people and of all nations. In due course the activation of SAARC will benefit the NEI and surrounding states through increased trade and commerce which are the engines of prosperity. The allegations of internal colonization are only desperate call of poverty and backwardness in outlook and lack of confidence. The same allegations of regional socialism were

trotted out against the central government of India by South Indian politicians. The conflicts arise due to uneven development of various states and sections of state population. The unevenness is natural in democratic progress depending on the quality of various executives. The uneven development is not due to any lopsided ambitions. In Assam, the immigrants took to commercial crops. The same can now be done by others and there is scope on account of expanding markets and globalization.

The Path of Progress

The path of Progress of any mixed society has to be based on peace and secularism. The ancillary requirements are of trained manpower, proper planning and investments. India has best tradition of peace and secularism and NEI is a welcome part of India. Globalization and development potential will attract the necessary investments provided the population of NEI gives evidence of accepting the basic conditions of peace and hard work and demonstrate confidence in themselves and others. India is willing to invest both capital and instructor organizations or their branches. The Indian Council of Industrial Research has already set up a regional research Lab at Jorhat and their work in spreading the cultivation of medicinal plants is note-worthy. The National Science Academy at Delhi had plans to set up an eastern branch in Assam but continued disturbances dissuaded some eminent scientists from volunteering at that time. Agricultural research is fairly advanced in India and extension centres can be opened in each district. The interested entrepreneurs should be allowed to import some key personnel if necessary. Those who materially contribute to the prosperity of NEI can be rewarded by grant of honorary citizenship in a locality of their choice. Every country in the world has used immigrant skills and investments. For attracting attention of outstanding outsiders, the NEI has to expand infrastructure,

communication and health facilities. Bengal, Bihar, Orissa, northern states of India who have often contributed to the education and culture of NEI have to show their heightened interest in the development of the region. This can be done by organized mutual visits for getting acquainted. Exchange of students and interns in national institutions should be fairly frequent.

Religion and Philosophy

The NEI need not travel along the complex route taken by the world at large in matters of religion and philosophy. They can jump across the centuries of darkness when people were innocent of modern science and the primacy of reason and logic. Marx has dubbed religion as the opium of the masses. Now most countries that claim to be democratic regard reform as undoing the imposed communist culture. The most advanced and most pragmatic philosophy is of co-existence and multiple beliefs allowing for the complexity of human mind. Secularism and humanism are the pragmatic religion and philosophy. These are also the basic tenets of Hindu religion. The Hindus consider tribal beliefs and traditions as good guides for the tribal people who naturally will advance in their beliefs. God and soul and the everlasting life of soul, are just linguistic contrivances as removed from reality as any other beliefs. We will take up the doctrines of *Karma* and rebirth, rather negate them for any active and forward looking society later.

NEI has been the cradle of Indian civilization. It was here that Hanuman, the non-human hero of Ramayana figured out the *Sanjivni* that revived the mortally wounded Lakshmana. NEI could directly adopt the development gospel of peace and fellowship. The tribal worship and beliefs are only the beliefs of tribal society of ancient Hindus. India is a fit background of further flowering of the tribal culture. More opportunities should be created for exchange of dance or cultural delegations from the NEI with other

states of India. This can demonstrate best the tribal culture at the base of whole of the country. Like the handicrafts of rest of the country, NEI crafts and designs can have a market in the whole world. The media coverage to NEI should be expanded to enlarge the understanding in the NEI of Indian innovative thought and design. The march forward has to be in step for the whole world. The new revolution is for steady progress in peace and friendship. The steady growth of UN governance and outlawing of wars with the strengthening of international security is the harbinger of the growth of one world. Now people are awake and aware that the earth as habitat of human beings is likely to last for another billion years, a time horizon never in the calculations of ancient philosophers who expected the judgement day around the corner. The human beings have the stage of the universe for their unhindered advance if only they consolidate peace and security of all human beings.

North east India and many other peripheral regions of ethnic discontent have now a clear goal of working for the humanist *mustopia* which seems to be the human destiny.

The New Paradigm for Beliefs—Mahayana

The author has named the new paradigm resting on humanism, democracy and coexistence—New Mahayana absorbing the popularity of the 1st century A.D. Buddhist faith of Mahayana that brought peace to the whole civilized world. Besides anchoring on the Buddhist eight-fold noble path, it also guaranteed freedom to have faith in any chosen God or gods. A belief in the one-ness of all creation need not be via a theistic belief in God but can be from the logic of survival of the human race through peace and progress. Human welfare and social justice should come to terms with religious call to service and to charity as the goal is the same of human evolution and happiness. We have every reason to be proud of our heritage from pursuit of religion. Could

the Ellora caves, the giant statue of Gomateshwara, myriads of temples and churches, or mosques of surpassing beauty, have been constructed right upto the modern times even if we do not count pyramids and temple hills constructed in the middle ages all over the old as well as the new world. A secular state is totally committed to democracy with special consideration of the welfare of the deprived. Exclusivist outlook and fanaticism is not specific to any religion. Tenaciously held non-religious beliefs can also lead to fanaticism. Maoism is almost vanished in China, its land of origin, but it is still a handy tool in the hands of Indian and Nepalese Marxists to cut asunder the peaceful posture of these states. The feeling that everything is known to a particular set of people and new insight or interpretation cannot occur is just childish. I once decided to go fishing on a Sunday, but on Saturday I was assured by a neighbourhood child that I will not catch any fish as all had been caught by him and his Pa that very day.

Such a tenacious almost fanatically held belief is theism and belief in an everlasting soul and its repeated re-births till salvation when it merges in God or is reduced to *shunya* or zero of the Buddhists. One must remember Lord Krishna with respect, wonder and awe that his proposition of rebirth and *Karma* theory is highly logical and product of reason in order to explain the diversity of a child's environment; no scientist can trust this theory. Alternative explanations have to be found for believed cases of apparent rebirth. Indians must get rid of this belief as it harms their efforts towards self-help in bettering their living standards and experimenting with their creativity. Doctrine of rebirth under-writes deterministic happenings while these are entirely subordinate to actions now of everyone. Let us not succumb to the poison of metaphysics, and of miracles. Life is to be lived with resolution and continuous improvement as in the oft-repeated Hindu prayer of the *Gayatri Mantra.*

Secularism

Secular outlook stands for inter-personal relations being based on ethics and morals and not on mutual labels of nationality, caste or creed. Dewey declared that morals are closest to human nature. One with a secular outlook is devoted to human welfare and pledged to human rights. The ancient Aryan formula in worship is an oft-repeated resolve for self-improvement. The propagation of secular outlook will proceed along with the spread of scientific outlook. Secular prayer or meditation places within the cherished monuments and museums like the Shinto shrines in Japan will spread the secular outlook so necessary for a multi-religious world. Any kind of worship has a respected place in a secular country. The global culture will be around secularism, humanism and tolerance and loving care of whole mankind. The policy of reaching democratic consensus will rid the world of tensions and allow it to progress in peace. Reason compels us to think of others and have respect for the rights of others. The increase of population, urbanization and contraction of space forces us to think of others. The peace and happiness of one must mean peace and happiness also of others.

Mahatma Gandhi emphasized that truth encompasses all religion. In the same sense, secularism and justice cover all aspects of civilized life. Labels of religion and caste must not determine our relations with others. A secularist is firmly established in truth and fellowship. Any progress requires knowledge and skill put to use for more production and income for leisure and self-culture. India boasts of a secular culture. From the times of the Vedas, we had theists, *advait vedantists* and atheists. Charvak propagated pure atheism with no belief in soul and rebirth. He had an able exponent in Osho so popular with modernists. Guru Nanak was a theist and combined the wisdom of the Buddhists and Jains with devotional theism. Indian and the Hindus' secular freedom to experiment with fresh ideas and attempt to reach

better plateau in thought. Humanism and secularism are basic in Hindu view of life. The *Ramayana* teaches steadfastness in promises. The formula leaves no room for violence and conspiracy.

Social Communication: Role of Tourism

Tourism develops exchange of ideas and is not something only for rich countries. The poor of India have indulged tremendously in tourism on foot. Even today, in a certain season young men start with empty pitchers on foot to distant towns on the Ganges to return with some Ganges water for offering to the idol in the local temple. In this exercise they walk on foot about three hundred kilometres. The travels kit is very brief and on the way they accommodate in markets that are empty at night and the philanthropic market places look after their meals suited to the time of the day. Most temples on the way are easy stops for few hours. Not only the Ganges, but other sacred rivers of the country also enthuse local young men in the same way. Bureaucratic red tape is normally unravelled when tourism and business combine. Bikaner is an out-landish corner town in Rajasthan. Local industry has popularized a widely known snack, fried noodles of gram flour. The town is connected to Delhi by an overnight train. If one wants to travel by this train, an amazing rapport is seen between railway staff including the driver and the guard of the train, the staff at road-side whistle stops and the passengers who all remember that they should not miss the chance to purchase the famous snack for their dear ones and guests at home. There is a snack vendor in the grab of a railway employee accosting you and even waking you up every few minutes until you have purchased few packets to take home. The train every night is a market on wheels for the supliers in Bikaner. Similar devices will have to be harnessed for creating and expanding the market for delicacies and art products of the NEI. There are not many trains and buses

entering NEI from outside. The few railway tracks terminate at some destinations in the area. Informally the railway trains at destination should double as tourist accommodation for one or two nights till its scheduled return journey. The railway staff when it is appointed in the NEI, may be permitted to cater to the passengers parked in the train for the return journey. The station master at the terminal station should be an authorized travel agent for elephant rides or other safaris starting from the terminal station. Similarly government servants that come in contact with the tourist passengers, be permitted to have a side business to serve tourism in some way or the other, by offering a view of the samples of jungle produce and locally produced wines in sealed bottles and sealed perfumes offered by local producers and trade.

Re-activation of society can be attempted through local festivals where a mobile display of various developments and outlines of new projects can be given. More people have learnt yoga in the Kumbh fairs than by classes conducted by teachers of Yoga. The fairs can be highly educative depending on their organizers. Nagaland proposes to organize a hornbill festival in winters. They have a tourist attraction in the form of a heritage village near Kohima. Limestone caves in Meghalaya, Tantrists and Yoni worshippers gather at Shaktipeeth near the Kamakhya temple at an Ambudri fair in July. Other famous sites near Guwahati are the Nabagriha temple and Vishwamitra Ashram.

3

Century of Preparation

Minimum Preparation

As the standard of life and standard of leisure activities rise and become uniform for large segments of society, the world will be on the road to *mustopia*. Training and educational facilities will be used throughout the day and throughout the year. Since the need of under-developed tribal population is greatest, every country and global institution will spare more time for them. Soon people will be ready for world citizenship and travel for advancement or recreation will become within the reach of the common citizen. The humanist economics will be on the rails and planners of every nation will exert to make a success of such economics that will end poverty and violent unevenness in the standard of life and recreation of the rich and the poor. India has already proclaimed a policy of providing remunerative work for all citizens. Same will be the routine policy in every nook and corner of the world. Only an educated, well-informed population can advance to the road of *mustopia*. Every nation has to seriously make everybody literate and educated. In the NEI and even in the whole of India full literacy is a far cry.

The whole population has to have sufficient income for housing, food and clothing. The necessary steps like humanist economics, universal activity to earn and save are already charted. India and the NEI have to actively work on

these issues. The NEI will get all the support from the national government. However, it is the people of the NEI who have to morally adopt the policy of peace and work towards a united economic zone of NEI and further extend it to wider zone involving West Bengal and Bangladesh which is now alert to the dangers of isolationist policies and aggressive postures. The minimum effort necessary for the income of every resident of the NEI is a good land use policy. Consolidation of holdings can be attempted by large scale clustering and cooperative movement. Ancillary industries to which every family can contribute like steps in silkworm rearing and utilization, bee-keeping and small patches of land to grow the aromatic and medicinal plants must multiply in the next couple of decades. Tea and timber economics must be organized in the interest of all concerned and particularly the inhabitants of the area.

India is diligently expanding the infrastructure of communications, learned institutes and extension services. The same must happen at greater speed in the NEI using local labour and skill augmented with imported ones of immigrants employed on fixed tenure (but promised permanent residence if their contribution is of the right quality). One incident of insurgency days is worth sharing, Jawaharlal Nehru University at Delhi was keen at one stage to open an Eastern Wing at Imphal. A team sent for preliminary discussion was told by agitating students in no uncertain terms that Manipur is keen for the centre to provide finance to them for setting up a Manipur University and not for setting up a branch of a Delhi University. The move was scuttled but this was an unwise step for a backward community as the direct link with a prestigious central university would have enriched the Manipur state as a matter of course in the design of courses, provision of educational technology and rotation of experts for teaching and research. The NEI must as a policy accept opening of branches and extension services by national institutions particularly scientific and technical institutions and services

that promote entrepreneurship, banking and trade. Human centred fiscal and monetary policies should prevail that brings forth the innovative skills of the population. The loans for development should be given after assessing the ability and working habits of the loan seeker and not on the mortgaging ability of land and tools.

Changes in Human Relations

Baha'Ullah gave the clearest call in recent times for people to get together their act for changing and transforming the world. A unified, just and peaceful world will result if people have commendable and seemly conduct and perform good deeds. The simplest rule is to feel the pleasure and pain of others. One has to enlarge one's horizon to include others with one-self. The whole world has to develop since it is man's destiny to flourish almost for ever on this earth. The stage is limited to earth's surface and he has the abilities and the time to either mar his future and destroy this habitat or nourish its gifts to make sustainable improvements in his environment, land and food resources and steadily improve the living standards of every human being. He has already seen how the standards of health, environment and well-being can improve for certain groups and how it will not be difficult to see such transformation in every nook and corner of the world. So far it was only the seers and prophets of various climes and epochs bearing witness to the necessity of spiritual progress of every person to bring about the condition of supreme bliss in the world for like believers. Now the whole world is itself moving in the direction of both scientific and moral advance. The scientific approach is forcefully brought before us only in the last few centuries since Newton, though empirical and halting progress in scientific knowledge and study of observations have been going on for a couple of millennia ever since the world had leisure to observe and meditate. The scientific propositions are based on experiments and observations and

are developed through reason and logic. These are quite convincing and the beauty is that scientists are ever happy with contradictions and improvements if new thinking can explain more observations or are more correct with regard to reasoning and logic. The signal for maturity of human civilization has only come recently with the advent of UN and its attempts at world governance. The more we can conform to the laws of social development and place more reliance on cooperative development of the whole world, the easier would it be to reach the steady path leading to *mustopia,* the goal and destiny of mankind.

The inter-personal relations determine the structure of society. We have come forward from feudalistic and high caste-low caste relationships and the wind now blowing is of equality, human rights, welfare and freedom to amass wealth through, trade, commerce or innovative production and service to others. In the brave new world where want will be banished and one has only to move ahead with friends in one's country or in the other countries. All are striving for the same result that of peace, and prosperity. Development and acquisition of wealth is no longer a zero-sum striving.

The wealth is created as people work on the natural resources and exercise their skill on whatever they work on. Even when the world was a madhouse of national ambitions, colonization and exploitation of the weak nations in their extended interest and jealous building of allies would help others develop. The USA was assisted by massive investments and migration of skilled man-power from Europe. The only other way was the way of regimentation found unsuccessful in the long run, but started with indigenous zeal and ultimate exercise in selfishness as did happen in case of Hitler's Germany and fascist countries of the right or the left. While the fascist or communist experiments were doomed to failure, countries like India and China who opted for mixture of neo-capitalism and welfare of all their populations have steadily progressed.

When asked a question, the Chinese assured the interlocutor that soon they would make more progress when some reforms, which were pending, were introduced. In their parlance reforms mean undoing whatever little vestige remains of communist regimentation in economic or social policies.

There seems to be some belief that tribals cannot get along with non-tribals. This must be shed under the realization that the whole world started in tribal formation. Some groups continue to be tribal, because they have been overpowered by their environment and could subsist only treating the traditions as sacred since these could somehow sustain them. The majority of people have moved out of tribal strait jacket by the chance happening of few proper leaders and intellectuals who could innovate and guide their fellows to easier or more abundant lives. Human beings have a sacred duty to neither exploit others nor allow others to exploit them. Exploitation starts when one is overpowered by desires and needs to seek loans from loan sharks. An essential feature of healthy economics is easy availability of loans and an assurance that the people are trustworthy and will return loans and interest in due course. This is possible now by the spread of rural banking under-written by government funds that help the individuals attempting to enhance their earnings.

More Teachers for NEI

Development is unthinkable in the absence of more education and training. The easy step is local reception of close by radio transmission channel devoted to development of skills, cooperative movement and guidance for peasant enterprises or handling of jungle produce, and help in marketing or procurement of raw materials and chemicals for treating soils or plants. The local reception should be on community sets at convienent evening time at suitable locations which will soon acquire the character of cultural

centres. The other method is to seek cooperation of advanced states in the neighbourhood. Suitable universities for example in UP, Bengal and Bihar may be prevailed upon to enroll students and teachers for short courses of about six weeks for some spoken language of NEI. The outside teacher who first has benefited from learning some spoken language of the NEI will be a good candidate for recruitment to a tenure teaching post in NEI. Such short term deputation will not harm the career of the teacher. During the deputation the teacher will continue to draw his usual salary and allowances from the new employer who will be re-imbursed by the government of India. Anyone including an outsider from another Indian state who is willing to invest his skill or funds should be encouraged to immigrate and set up his small scale industry in NEI preferably in partnership with some local enthusiast. Even coaching entrepreneurs are coming from Japan and opening teaching shops in Delhi for bright kids preparing for competitive tests for admission to professional technical institutions.

Self-Help

Self-confidence and self-help will go far towards development of the NEI. The regeneration of self-help in a climate of cooperation with others is going to be entirely successful. The schooling and gathering knowledge and improving one's skills will have automatic priority. Conclusions reached by science will be continuously accepted till further scientific advance occurs. Superstitions and trust in magic and magical cures will be whittled down with simultaneous wider reach of integrated medicine. National and regional steering committees will look after the progress of all major projects. Charities will be supervised nationally and a climate of security for the workers and volunteers created. Creativity and entrepreneurship is the key to progress. High science and technology will be harnessed for the welfare of farmers and for land management. Most of entertainment

will be voluntary in fairs and festivals. The temples, churches and historical and congregational spots will come alive for all irrespective of tribe, caste or creed.

What the Tribals Can Contribute

The establishment of the *mustopia* is the goal of society and desirable even for the most primitive groups. The NEI will have lots to contribute especially because of their familiarity with English, which will be the chief vehicle of transformation of society and environment. Tourism especially with planned exposure of hard pressed business tycoons and bankers to wild life of the jungle, simple life in a north east village, and healthy sport and dance spectacles will be popular worldwide including adventurous stay for a few days for the foreign teenager in rejuvenated tribal bachelor halls. Tourism will spread customary tribal politeness and care for the weaker sex. The Manipuri dance extravagances, the scenic beauty of Arunachal Pradesh, and adventure treks along rivers will give a new enthusiasm to the NEI along with more riches and friendships. The Bodo land's hospitality, Assam's delicate cuisine and inter-state fellowship of India will favour travel to the NEI, the fountain-head of ancient Hindu tribal culture.

What Central Indian Planning Could Do

India is vitally interested that as soon as possible all parts of the country became prepared to travel on the *mustopia* road. The people of the NEI living in many past centuries existing side by side can provide answers to many problems connected with multiple societies and their development. The central government may have to devise time framed social development projects for international study. Indian institutes of higher science and technology should have few seats reserved for NEI students who make the grade. The museums should have separate sections depicting arts and

crafts of NEI which will also help in advancing such designs. Rule of law and peaceful resolution of all problems will be propagated by all means. Any government servant accused of law breaking regarding secularism and welfare of people would be severely dealt with. Public or private contributions for welfare should be in the form of financing schools, hostels, and dispensaries for the public. The Naga clan chiefs and the present keepers of traditional customs should be exalted by conferring appropriate honorific titles (when they also understand modern insistence on secularism and human rights) to be honoured by all. At government co-sponsored fairs and inaugurations, camps for teaching yoga and screening of selected Indian short films of scenic sights and pilgrim spots should be held. India should not rest just with allocating of funds but involve trustworthy agents to see that there is no scam or wastage.

What Bengal Can Do

The NEI will develop according to its wishes and within its competence. Bengali speaking population of the NEI can help in many ways, once the recently raised barriers of language and script are forgotten. The schools teaching in Bengali should also accommodate Assamese or some other local NEI language. Bengal state of India should grant suitable technical scholarships to Bengali speaking aspirants from NEI. There are many basic scientific and technical institutions in Bengal and an internship there for about a year will equip them to become leaders of science and technology in NEI. Few chairs of NEI literture, anthropology and sociology could be instituted in Bengal institutions to increase scholarship and research for the advances in the areas useful to the NEI. The growing strength of SAARC will induce Bangladesh to shed *jehadist* influences and decide to march with rest of the world towards the path of *mustopia.* They will find natural allies in Indian West Bengal and the NEI. An important step towards trade and commerce in

South and South East Asia can be the opening up of communication links between the NEI and West Bengal across Bangladesh. Pakistan and India have re-started the rail and bus links between the two countries as means for future peace and progress. The lesson cannot be lost on Bangladesh. The communist leadership in India, Bengal and Bangladesh and other neighbouring states can see the writing on the wall. Both China and India when they use approvingly the word "reforms", they mean undoing the vestiges of communist and socialist planning that they earlier had started. West Bengal is unique in experimenting and approving the joint Hindu-Muslim culture of 19th century Bengal. The same has a bright future for whole of South Asia. The economics of all countries is introducing private enterprise widely. The communist doctrinaire working class revolt is smothered by welfare economics and neo-capitalism induced growth. Future belongs to democracy, protection of human rights and the road to *mustopia.*

Naga Culture

Naga tribes were the metal workers who enriched Indian exports of metal-ware of ancient Bengal along with metal works from central India. They practiced various arts and decorated the morungs (youth dormitories) by zoomorphic designs (women were debarred from entering morungs). In the same village more than one language could be spoken. Same language group was known as *khel.* As a child every girl learnt spinning, weaving and dyeing. They celebrated a Moatse (Sanskrit : Maha-utsav) festival of general merriment. Most disputes were settled by the payment in the form of cattle. Witchcraft is rampant.

They traded or bartered what they could collect of jungle produce for essentials like salt etc. with the plains people. The British also arranged market places for them to use in order to avoid their descent on other villages who may not be ready for trade. They also brought horticulture

and herbi-culture products. Most trade was in the hands of Marwaris and Manipuris. The state governments can easily increase commerce and trade including exports by improving communications and creating banking and insurance facilities. There was never a conflict between planters and the old ruling class. The value base of the tribal folk is still in tact. There is opposition to the spread of Christianity in Arunachal Pradesh, but Nagas in general are Christians and have benefited for the activities of the Christian missionaries. The social assemblies like Panchayats can take cognizance of disputes and inflict punishment like social ostracism. The social system in the NEI did not change except for Christians. Individuals celebrate festivals of merit but the assemblies of Nagas have abolished this custom.

Assamese Culture

The Assamese culture is Bengali culture in food and dress but attached to Assamese language and literature. Bengalis constitute about one-fourth of the population and live in amity with the Assamese. Most Assamese learn Bengali too. Assam is mainly the Brahmaputra valley and the Cachar valley. Surma valley residents prefer to be counted as Assamese. Jaintia and Khasi speak common language Mon Khmer and are now in the new state of Meghalaya. They worship any deities including Hindu deities. A Khasi high priest is known as Lyngdoh. By the end of the 20th century about a dozen tea plantations were owned by the Assamese. The first Assamese tea planter was Mani Ram. He was a martyre in 1858 and his tea plantation was confiscated. The heads of tribal clans are known as Bakhrawas.

The Khasis excelled in smelting iron and their metal objects were items of export, which declined with the rise of imports from Britain. Last Khasi rebellion ended only in 1833 against imperial encroachment on Khasi land. Urbanization was started by the British with the establishment of a new

civil station at Chera and a township at Shilla on the route to Sylhet. Shillong was a flourishing town in 1866. A high school was upgraded to a college in Shillong in 1971. The education is in both Bengali and Assamese languages. Political movements were generally revivalist and reformist. The Khasi middle class and education overcame the traditional power sytem. Landed aristrocarcy was absent. Capitalists from outside invested in business and trade. The British were attracted by the forest wealth of Assam. The masses opted quickly for sedentary agriculture. The silk industry is well developed. Only now the immense economic potential is likely to receive the attention it deserves. So far local leaders were at logger heads with the Indian government to the issue of sharing profits of development before the profits started to arrive. The state can help in globalization as Indonesia has done in Bali. Tradition can become part of modernity. The Nagas form a community prone to global values of individuality and consumerism.

Manipur

Manipur has advanced agriculture. It is the home of paradise flowers. There is a floating National park at Keipule. It has about 100,000 industrial units. Its exports include cement and textiles. Biggest setback is in the disruption of communications with Bangladesh. The communication via Guwahati means extra thousands kms of road journey. There is a centre for Electrical Design and Development at Imphal, the chief town of Manipur. A railway terminus has come up in Manipur in 1990. Moreh is the Manipur centre for the drugs trade. There is a national highway connecting Imphal with Silchar in Assam.

The Central NEI ministry should shift to Manipur for opening direct channels of commerce with Bangladesh and Myanmar through SAARC.

Nagaland

Nagaland was declared a separate state of India in a compromise ending the rebellion of the Nagas which had been simmering ever since the colonial days. Nagaland comprised the compact Naga areas on the border with Myanmar. The Naga resistence to the spread of British colonial control over the Naga areas was quite insistent. The grant of statehood to a population of mere 500,000 Nagas was a constitutional aberration since the bill for having a legislature, cabinet and a governor would cost crores of rupees to the new state or its backer like the central government of India. The Nagas financed their rebellion by exploitation of peaceful neighbours and waging war on civilians outside Nagaland. Insurgency and counter insurgency of Nagas and Mizos ruined the area and government decision pacified both by letting them have their autonomous states and create legitimate funds to govern their territories. All the new states of the NEI are endowed with natural resources and nature's gifts. The shortcoming is acute in modern education and skills that alone can help the newly created middle class and central development efforts to bear fruit. The government of India has created in 2001 a central ministry at Delhi to assist in the development projects in the NEI. The governance must be streamlined, by giving state powers to an elected district governor in each district with state and centre's advice to create funds for development projects especially concerning education and imparting of business and management skills. A priority must be to manage forests for sustainable output. Timber factories with poor forest management will impoverish the land fast. Politics of homelands will not solve NEI problems. The land grab has hurt the Nagas who were dependent on the forests for hunting and food gathering. Reconciliation is the best answer to Nagaland-Manipur differences. Jamir's pamphlet Bedrock ridicules fanciful history sought to be believed by the Nagas. The only contact between remote isolated Naga

villages was head hunting, one brave stalked and killed another one who was unaware. Still, the Naga values of discipline, honesty and hard work will certainly help them succeed. In Nagaland there is already 100 per cent rural electrification.

Mizoram

The Mizos also staged a violent campaign for their own separate state and since India was engaged on demarcation of states on linguistic principle, the state of Mizoram was conceded to end ethnic vigilantism perpetrated by the Mizo National Front. The establishment of homelands was reducing democracy and ignored the well-being of ethnic minorities in the new state, but it was felt that new responsibilities of the state will grant them wisdom to create conditions of rule of law and a feeling for growth and development. The expectations have been well met in both Mizoram and Arunachal Pradesh, which are on the road to peaceful progress. The population has gone up by 50 per cent in the past twenty years. A link was between politicians and rebels. Mizoram excels in horticulture and sericulture. Cash crop of ginger is grown. Mizoram desires its border to be fenced with Nagaland.

Assam

Assam is one of the most beautiful states of India. The British colonial regime was interested in acquiring Assam and were prepared to go to war with Myanmar for it. The Assamese love music and singing. The traditional flute 'Siphong' is popular. Dr. Hazarika's song 'Bohag' composed in 1890 knitted together many Assamese. The Assam agitations were not anti-national but only against illegal entry of refugees from both Bengals as well as others. It is now official policy to identify such immigrants and to deport them elsewhere. Despite some dissent, the Assam civil society pursues its

patriotic agenda chalked out by Bardoloi of Indian freedom struggle. The AASU was swept to strength because of the perceived slow pace of development and inconsequential return from the use of Assam's natural resources. The tribes in Assam do not favour any melting pot ideas but want to preserve their culture. From 1990, the middle class has experienced siege mentality from the posturing of the minority tribes. ULFA which fought for Assamese independence is now integrationist in outlook. The rule of law and basic freedoms in the present truncated Assam will redeem its fortunes as a result of industrialization and development well on its way.

People would prefer an end to diarchy when the governor and the chief minister do not work together. India has to get involved with the progress in the NEI, but it is better to stay away from administration. Rule of law and assured basic rights will redeem the fortunes of the truncated Assam. The poet and nationalist leader Ambika Roy Chaudhury favoured multi-national states in the NEI, but with failure of the Soviet Union, the recipe favoured by the communists has blown away. Many politicians see elements of diarchy in the powers conferred on the chief minister and the governor. For economy one can suggest that the entire NEI should be governed district-wise by an elected Siem or chief with a nominated panel of advisers for police and justice, for planning and development, education and commerce etc. All charity, grants and government funds must pass through the chief who will be held responsible for all expenditure. The plans will not be an occasion of jubilation or media hullabaloo, but only completion of projects and results would be subject of media attention. ULFA and SULFA will fade away as ugly dreams. Hazarika's songs have shown the power of public acceptance and vigilence against intruders. India should minimize its attention to administration and have only a guiding role in this. Many festivals are held in the Bihu season. Meghalaya grows cash crops of oranges, oil seeds, cashew nuts and

coffee. They have expanded their iron and steel industry. There is uranium to be mined in Khasi hills.

Internally Displaced Persons

There are a large number of displaced persons within the NEI. About 100,000 Bengalis were uprooted in Tripura in 1993, 130,000 Kukis were displaced in Manipur in 1952 and Brues and Reangs were expelled from Mizoram. A US committee reports 157,000 internally displaced persons in the NEI. Chakmas are displaced from Arunachal. It is surmised that 50 per cent of displaced persons are children. This is a colossal task of rehabilitation. Each district should volunteer to share the task along with philanthropic and other state and central organizations. Any selected individuals out of displaced persons should be recruited for a national police and volunteer force and billeted in various districts in the NEI and outside. India is already faced with similar problem in the J&K state and in Bihar and Tamil Nadu states. Nepali residents invited there on tenure basis are now displaced in Meghalaya. Many countries of the world have used Indian peasants for their farming and construction works. India should formally assist in providing safe haven for our internally displaced persons by arranging remunerative work for them in the better off states of India or outside. The NEI is the last frontier of land hungry persons in India but here were still some open places in the world where able bodied persons are in short supply. In some districts 85 per cent of recruitment is restricted to SC and ST classes. Such a condition should not stand in the way of special needs of development projects. Any outsider including government servants who devotedly serve in the NEI may be allowed to apply for citizenship if they have the necessary skill or capital to contribute for starting some business or enterprise in association with a local entrepreneur. Political parties should emphasize their civic agenda and not ethnic partiality. Bardoloi in 1986 found

actual ownership of land to be with Bengalis and Nepalis while nominal ownership was of aboriginees. This should be regularized so that all live in honour and confidence. An active welfare state equally happy if development is carried out by private or public enterprise is the only solution. An Asia centre for human rights at Delhi pursues the situation in this respect. Conflict induced displacement has to be addressed by the quarrelling society by being forced to bear the cost of rehabilitation. Proliferation of autonomous districts for meeting partially the home land demands is no solution. The solution is to be found in co-existence, *Sarvodaya* or global society of peaceful progress.

Inter-State Communications

The colonial rule disrupted old trade routes to Nepal, Tibet, Bhutan and Myanmar. Assam-Yunnan route across Patkoi range became out of use. There was a tenuous link with Tibet (Dzong and Tawang) which was used by the Dalai Lama when he fled from Chinese occupation from Lhasa to India. The town of Haja in Assam was the hub of the mini silk route to China. Khasi cinnamon export to China was using this route. With the growing links of India and South East Asian countries there is hope that there will be created partial free trade and mini economic zones involving NEI and some Asian countries. Khasi industrial zone in Meghalaya can be the manufacturing and commercial zone of such expected trade in India and the financial and multi-national globalization centre remaining at Singapore. Communications across Bangladesh should be re-started as a zonal contribution to the prosperity of the countries on the borders of India in the east. The prospects of increased trade and educational exchanges and transfer of investment funds are indeed bright. This will also open up the tourist potential in the NEI and pilgrim traffic across Bangladesh to Assam and Myanmar. Yunnan's historical role of transit trade between India and South East Asia can be restored by

reopening of the old Ledo road (Stillwel road). This will require only less than 100 km long road in India and Myanmar and to increase the usage of the road, a new pontoon bridge can be built across the Irrawati river in Myanmar. The old bridge was destroyed in 1947 as a security measure. Asia highway also needs the construction of a couple of short links. This is only a challenge to diplomacy of China and India. Perhaps they can attend to this after slow completion of the boundary accord between these Asian countries. The first step should be to banish any remaining traces of fundamentalism notably in Bangladesh, Nagaland and Manipur. There should be soft border to these countries for the promotion of tourism which will benefit the whole world and also the income starved countries of the region. Home-land aspirations are suicidal for most of the groups living in the NEI. The future lies in the principles of co-existence, globalization and peaceful development.

4

Development for Tribal Population

Development Costs

Development costs for bringing the tribal population to minimum modern standard of regular rural population is not much for a large country like India. Any allocations will be cost effective. The inexpensive part is allowing them freedom in their villages and in the forests. Literacy campaign should penetrate their forest dwellings and a local community receiver should be provided for each 100 population. The community receiver should be the centre of community meet practically every evening for the promotion of literacy and culture. Centuries old stagnation has been rent asunder by the tribal population themselves when they were ready to rebel against the perceived threat of dispersion and starvation. District development councils should be set up with adequate resources for the local population. Each month a tribal fair should be held at government cost using the gathering for promoting yoga, ways of earning extra income for men and women using the proximity of forests and their skill in weaving and making artifacts from straw and cane and silk cocoons. The traditional leaders should be given modern titles which will bring more respect to democratic leadership. An honorific title should be invented for all Naga youth when they come of age like *subedar ji*. The old structure of young teen agers' life can be revived by rebuilding at government expense the

youth dormitories with facilities for primary education and education regarding *mustopia*. Enlightenment sections can be set up to provide information and guidance of use to the illiterate forest dwellers including literacy and knowledge about their tribe and the country. Elements of and advantage of settled agriculture and animal husbandry can be driven home. Herbal agriculture can catch on with some direct interest of officials and the elders.

North East and Immigrants

All immigrants will be registered with the district authorities and stay for a specified period for an allotted task. Only the children of immigrants who have Indian citizenship by birth will have voting rights. The laws regarding land transfer will be strictly followed. Tribal land cannot be purchased by an immigrant. Immigrants do become owners by benami transactions, but for any land use they better work in a deal with a local person who will be regarded as the owner. In Myanmar all businesses that are started with immigrants as partners are legally owned by a citizen of Myanmar. Same terms can be adopted for tribal NEI. On the expiry of residential permit, the immigrant will have to leave the district and move elsewhere with the approval of government. An immigrant like a teacher or scientist or entrepreneur who has served the NEI well may if he/she so desires get the residential permit extended. State and central government employees will get preference for residential permits especially if they can invest their skills or administrative or scientific acumen in the NEI. The immigrant worker engaged on a development project would be made welcome and allowed to intermingle with the local population. Each district will determine the annual immigration quota if any. Any blanket denial to immigration can be against the district's interest. The immigrants in responsible positions will be required to have a local under-study for eventual replacement of the immigrant.

Citizenship and Human Rights

Citizenship is acquired by birth or as stipulated in laws of the country. All residents may not be voters but all have same freedoms as other citizens. They, while in India will have freedom of religion or belief and allow the same freedom to other residents. This means ready fellowship in cultural and social activities of all residents so long as they do not rub others especially the tribal population on the wrong side. All residents are also world citizens along with other Indians. India is already a *mustopia* so far as personal beliefs and intellectual fancies are concerned. The folk of NEI have all the opportunity to interpret the past civilization of the tribals and other Indians. Indian thought is a continuous spectrum from Tribal beliefs and myths to monotheism, atheism and pantheism with robust branches of anarchism, materialism, and noble deeds etc. Buddhism and Jainism have been there from Vedic times and there has been exchanges going on in each theology and philosophy. But all are against fanaticism. They swear with pluralism and coexistence. This is a common feature of ancient civilizations. Rural China believes in tribal ghosts, Hindu-Buddhist deities, Confucianism and advanced mental constructs. In Greece, the role of reason was higher than that of sectarianism. In Peru, Christianity embraces ancient beliefs that existed before the death grasp of inquisition. India has only praise for the preachers and missionaries who have made contributions to the re-awakening of India.

India is for freedom in the exercise of human rights. One right is the right to gainful employment. India has made provision for old age pensions and stipends to women who have passed their prime in service to their families. An important concept is of *"Karseva"* or self-less service and in the same category is the constructive work so essential for the uplift of any people. Any worker voluntarily deciding to stay in NEI would be an asset for the education and skill

starved lands. Certain communities of India like Sindhis and Marwaris excel particularly in entrepreneurship of special variety like marketing, trade, banking or tourism. Entrepreneurs from anywhere should be welcome particularly if they come with finances and skills for some chosen industrial or training project. Punjabi farmers are in demand everywhere for bringing back fertility to the soil and for intensive farming.

Education for Sarvodaya

Modern India as well as future *mustopia* believes in *sarvodaya,* the doctrine of development favoured by Mahatma Gandhi. *Sarvodaya* is very much concerned with the verdict of total analysis that combines value analysis with engineering system analysis concerned with the feasibility and profitability studies. Any development which does not promote the well-being of the poorest of the land can wait. In NEI, since average income and standard of life is low, there is no accumulation of capital, no educated middle class and poor facilities for developing useful skills, the primary concern would be literacy and practical instruction in traditional skills like weaving and wood carving. The NEI has the advantage of widespread familiarity with the English language, an international language for industry, medicine and management. Literacy would mean elementary education in English too. In the NEI, familiarity with Bengali will help in social integration and dispel the estrangement from illegal immigrants from Bangladesh. When the multinationals become more active in SAARC countries, Bengali initiatives for management and adminsitration are going to be an asset to NEI.

Development of the rural folk follow the guaranteed remunerative work to all. Such guarnatee is already applicable to certain districts of the Punjab. For any constructive work, social acceptance must first come from the rural environment and any necessary workers from

outside would deserve social acceptance during their contribution to the constructive efforts. Physical welfare, peace and easy communications like telephone connection for every village or stack of villages and easy availability of electrical power are necessary. In Soviet Russia the slogan for development was electrification. The electrification will bring about many new enterprises. Maintenance of the electrification will require large number of maintenance staff. At least diploma level education in engineering must become widespread. The teaching can be in the local languages provided the technical and scientific vocabulary is bodily lifted from English. The students and teachers must resolve to contribute some work to the fruition of *Sarvodaya* efforts. The living costs for students can be quite low and met by the stipends that most of them will get and by restarting the youth dormitory system. This will also make health and hygiene education easy and at practically no cost.

Sarvodaya includes care of women especially through a sense of gene equality. Gene partiality has been usual in NEI as in the rest of India. The Christian missionaries have already made a dent in female illiteracy, but much more has yet to be done. Some diploma courses particularly for women can be started around silk and weaving. Simple lessons in commerce and trade can be imparted on the radio for women. Men, women and children should benefit from the application of computers to all business and management.

Education in Science and Technology

Science education is basic for any country to take to development. Elementary education in science is best through first raising the curiosity of the students and then giving the scientific explanation. Such basic education in science is also necessary for the illiterate adults through radio and public talks and exposition of scientific discourses. The colleges of education should not shrink away from introducing high science and new technologies especially

the advent of nuclear energy which will soon augment energy resources of each district. Experimental kits have been designed to help the teachers in science education. Most techniques invented in the course of learning high science are such as can be usefully employed in development of agriculture, health, commerce and banking. Geology and biology are subjects more within grasp of common sense and need more ability in classification and observation. The first thing that Nehru did for science education in the country besides getting them to start IITs and the national laboratories was to set up about two hundred fellowships for study of geology at graduate level and above. The other major effort with the cooperation of British experts was to provide for a hundred stipends each year for advanced study and training overseas particularly in American Universities. Similar efforts within the financial resources of the state and of Indian industry have to be started for the NEI.

Modern age is known as the age of computers. Computers can assist man in every job, pastime or data processing. Mini computers are now associated with telephone hand sets. Computers and radio-television are important for the spread of information and knowledge. The user is often instructed by the computer itself how to put it to use for his particular aim. Users of new devices are at an advantage since they need not pursue the earlier zig-zag path to reach the capacity of modern gadgets. Instruments and computers can create new melodies, poetry and songs, diagnosis of diseases, and suggest medical prescriptions. Like the true Akash Vani (divine statement) of the ancient faith, all knowledge is within reach, only one has to have an internet connection. Technological miracles are no less than the spiritual ones. The real spiritual miracles are in the blossoming of a rare genius in some area or the other. Technological miracles are different. These require some machines or apparatus, usually an electrical connection and presto, things can be made to happen even by a child following set instructions. These things that happen are

much beyond the capability of any unaided man or god. Television, telephone, radio, remote sensing, artificial limbs, spectacles for better eyesight, laser conducted bloodless operations; many medical wonders are all such miracles. A citizen of NEI can also perform these miracles after some effort at education and learning science and technology or the ability to purchase knowledge and skills for which also riches, through trade and commerce, use of natural resources by further working on them and by intelligent management of the skills, the people possess, are necessary.

5

Justice and Law

Introduction

Love of justice is an essential element of humanism. Indian civilization is primarily humanist and secular. The dogma of rebirth and reaping of results of deeds performed in earlier birth arose out of Indian pre-occupation with justice. The only way to account for uneven conditions at birth was to ascribe these to soul's good or bad deeds in a previous existence on this earth. Now that world has advanced in science and is fully aware that there can be no soul separate from the human body and that there is no believable proof of rebirth, we have to look to other causes of uneven conditions at birth. In case the parents are economically or otherwise well off, the new born baby is going to progress normally and if they are in indifferent circumstances, it is going to have to struggle to reach its appropriate maturity. The genes that the baby inherits from his parents and ancestors do influence its capabilities and given suitable rearing and growth there is good chance of it becoming a mature and useful member of society. It is the social organizaton that determines the relative prosperity and self-confidence of the parents. We have to build a society in which all have reasonable standard of life and each child has the facility for its natural growth and can give expression to its natural and acquired talents and abilities. Some of the social inability can be overcome by the grit of parents and the child itself. In the bye-gone days when "might is right"

prevailed and hereditary inferiority and superiority was expressed everywhere, the child had to rely only on chance encounter of a friendly lord and master. Now, however, things are changed, everyone can in principle advance to the extent his innate ability and that of his friends and teachers can assist. Thus injustice to the new born child, we have to build a society of equality and one that has respect for human rights for all. In addition diligent efforts have to be made to provide efficient schooling and training to free the child of all worries regarding its future.

Karl Marx has rightly observed religion to be the opium of the people. The priests of every religion want the people to resign to the will of the Lord. How can a benevolent and mighty Lord be all nice to one child and indifferent to another. The religion that teaches acceptance of one's position of undeserved inferiority should give way to a religion that stimulates people to make extra effort to improve their status and reach normal heights of achievement on account of one's innate abilities and devotion to own ideals and by service to others. The *mustopia* way is continuous sharpening of one's faculties in cooperation with others for material as well as inner happiness. For justice to prevail, the land has to be governed well. Evil inclinations have to be curbed, if necessary, by courts of law where judges can act fearlessly. The judges have to proceed according to law of the land. If there are lacunas in the law, justice will not win. A corollary to all this is that every effort should be made to codify and simplify the law. India is still away from a codified personal law applicable to all (since it will be constructed to cover all situations). The tribal councils can do this task for covering all the tribes who constitute half the population of NEI. It will then be easy to extend that code and modify where necessary to cover others who are not tribal. A school of law should be established that encodes law and publicizes the coded laws.

Law and Land Allocations

The discriminatory traditions regarding rights in land should be liquidated in view of the overriding national interest in equal rights of all unless special favours are extended and included in the law books to some on account of their superior service to the national development. The special rights will not extend to progeny. Gender discrimination even when it has its origin in traditions ought to be liquidated. There should be equality among men and women for all elections, e.g. elections to panchayats or executive advisory bodies. The district and state officials have to work within the law whether the application is for private utilization or official utilization. Naturally, some priority will have to apply for needs of tribal institutions functioning within the law of the land. The land is the primary resource for tribal life. The legal authorities must find a way to thwart benami sales of land to outsiders where the source of livelihood of a tribal family is threatened. Forests are to be managed in the national interest keeping the interest of the tribal persons secure when they have been dependent on that land. The NEI must be given due share of the income that others may derive after creating wealth from land, minerals or hydro-electric power derived from a resource of tribal origin. The water that flows out of NEI and becomes a material conferring wealth from the skilful use by others should carry back some royalty to the land of origin.

Immigration and Emigration

Any immigrants who have entered under false pretences must be externed on detection. This must be done unobtrusively. It has already been made clear that certain immigrants will always be necessary when proper quality experience has yet to be created. The Nepalese and some Bangladeshis were employed for specific purpose which they carried out for the prosperity of NEI. If their children

born in India are still settled in the NEI, they should be allowed residence and in due course the voting rights. Persons with desired skills should be allowed to enter on tenure jobs. If necessary, immigration quotas for special categories of workers may be fixed taking a cue from the immigration system of the USA. As a special case even Indian citizenship will not automatically permit Indians from outside to settle in the NEI. This will be a relic of the inner line policy perfected in the pre-independence days. They would however be welcome to do so if they bring in required skills, required investment funds, and the scarce commodities of entrepreneurship and creativity. The decision of the district authorities would be final and may have to be revalidated after five years. Tourist and transit visas will be made relatively cheaper and easier. Entry visas for students, artists, explorers and scientists will be easily given if the visitor has financial independence or assurance from a reliable provider of funds.

Any volunteer or a voluntary organization desiring to work for the fight against poverty and stagnation of NEI will be allowed to do so preferably in association with a similar NGO already active in these parts. From the experience of other parts of the country, the middle class and vociferous activists will grow fast in the NEI. It is up to the district authorities to give them constructive work and facilities allowed by the central and state governments. They can become change agents developing cooperative movement, banking, organizing small businesses and teaching in small groups. Any volunteer teacher who is competent and wishes to settle in the difficult conditions may be facilitated. The NEI could organize and finance cultural troupes to visit rich cities of India, South Asia and the West to raise funds for the NEI. Such troupes are to be held together when abroad and brought back to the NEI. This will require help from Indian embassies stationed overseas. The handouts and tourist literature distributed by the cultural troops when aborad will project the NEI to

become a prolific resource of international commerce and tourism. The government should assist any students or emigrants desirous of working overseas. The special attainments of NEI tribal people and others would make them ideal immigrants for labour starved northern Europe or large cities of India. The people can be given short training in simple jobs and work like care-takers, attendants for children, or helpers in hospitals. The NEI must run an insurance scheme that can look after their repatriation after completion of business contracts. The government of India can provide them when overseas about four weeks vacation per year if they agree to spend the vacation at some designated craft place for improving their own skill in that line. The NEI and the government of India would also institute about fifty stipends fully covering passage both ways and all student expenses if the persons selected work or study at designated places to be arranged by the Indian embassies or directly by the efforts of the applicant for a minimum period of six months and a maximum period of one year. Whenever possible, the authorities will help them secure appropriate employment on return. The NEI entrepreneurs or enterprise managers will have the opportunity to sponsor any stipend holder from start or to select one already undergoing training abroad in which event they could guide the student in correct direction when amassing training and experience.

Transnational Affinity

The NEI is situated on the cross roads between India, Bangladesh, Bhutan, China, Myanmar and further east to Thailand and Java. They must reawaken their cultural and business relations with the outside countries and get out of a well of their own creation. Hindus of India are arisen in part from immigrants from north and east across the NEI. Many tribes in the lands outside have intimate clan relations with the tribes in the NEI. In the brave new world on the

path to *mustopia and global citizenship,* these affinities will give the residents of the NEI a larger stage to demonstrate their talent for steadfast pursuit of happiness in their tribal faith. Even the intruder Bengali population among them will be an asset by providing linguistic and business underpinning. Special institutes for teaching Assamese or Bengali or English should be started to give short intensive courses for desirous adults. Ethnicity can be a bridge in place of a handicap when nations have succeeded in living together in peace and cooperation.

Lawlessness

Law has arisen out of traditions. The traditions in one tribe may be different from those of another. Law is created so that it can be accepted for interpersonal relations by all the residents. The base for all law is humanism and secularism. Humanism assures equal regard for all human beings and secularism equal regard for all gods and beliefs. Primitive life was succeeded by the principle of 'might is right' when life was entirely dependent on one's own cleverness and strength. This situation led to continuous strife. In order to achieve peace and stability, people paid attention to preachers of love and fellowship. Altruism, self-fulfilment through charity, good deeds and feeling pain of others were discovered as alternative systems of mutual interaction. Chaitanya Mahaprabhu's movement of Vaishnavism spread from Bengal, Bihar and Orissa to NEI and had a great reception there. Many parts of Bengal and NEI harbour strong attraction to this religion of love and fellow feeling. It is the whole world which is now slowly succumbing to the doctrine of love. As soon as the people everywhere accept the truth that earth is going to be human habitat almost for ever and there is nothing that can thwart people everywhere from marching forward on the road to *mustopia* together in peace. Sky would be the limit for abundance and happiness of people and the world will be breathing in unison. All

nations, big and small, ethnic groups on the borders or in the recesses of hinterland, will progress in cooperation.

The United Nations to which all nations surrendered a part of their sovereignty will assure absence of internal or external violence. The laws will enshrine human rights and secularism. UN governance will curb piracy, international drug traffic, cruelty to weaker sections and other crimes beyond the capacity of nations acting alone. The principle of New Mahayana, *i.e.* coexistence of all gods, all nations and all isms has been discovered and woven into all laws. Human mind has a canvas which is wide enough to attend to even contradictory theories to make them give way to coexistence or comprehensive sum. The matters are now to be processed in the crucible of experience, and scientific approach of applying reason and logic. In ancient India, the propositions were defended or criticized peacefully in public through reason and proven experience. Our common law will have to accommodate many binding beliefs for certain groups. There will however be a genuine effort to reform and simplify law and to jettison the garbage which may be weighing down the believers. Once I had accidentally while climbing a ladder on the side of a ship at sea slipped into the sea while still holding the iron ladder. Very soon I realized that the ladder that was meant to help me climb out of the sea, was now weighing me down to sink in the ocean, and I released my hold on the iron ladder; the ladder sank and I surfaced from where my friends guided me to climb out to ship's deck.

The humanist economics will look after old people and the handicapped. In *mustopia* everyone will have a memory of happy childhood among loving crowd of people including doting parents and happy siblings. The skills of everyone will have a chance to make their mark. Women will get equal rights in law as well as in practice. Laws of heredity will be modified to assure that means of production continue to be well managed. The climate of joy and cooperation will prevail all over the world as in a happy family. Hinduism

as prevalent in India is tolerant and respects diversity, which has real merit for world unity. It was very interesting to learn that certain tribal folk in Indonesia, afraid of the majority imposition in religion and philosophy elected to be classified as Hindus when they found that they could exercise maximum of religious security and regard from other citizens (of Indonesia) who were mostly Muslims or Christians. This is quite interesting that normally Hindus do not believe in religious conversion since all human beings belong to ancient Hinduism, a religion of humanism and continuous reform to be in tune with new advances in knowledge and in society.

Once the NEI has carried out some of the steps outlined above, it can expect to be counted among nations and ethnic groups emerging on the road to *mustopia* and on the bandwagon of continued peace and progress. The NEI will in fact lead India and the world in many ways.

6

Humanist Development

Introduction

NEI is proceeding in peace towards slow and steady progress. The governments of the states and centre with its new ministry of NEI are engaged on various nation building and development projects. Democracy seems to be taking root. However, the development should remain humanist in outlook and in substance. Humanist development is essential element of *Sarvodaya* so necessary for reasonably happy life for all. The value of humanist economics has already been stressed. However, if land is taken away from a person or from the community living at subsistence level mainly on the bounty of the land, water or the forest cover, alienation of land is a calamity.

In a humanist dispensation alternative rehabilitation of the dispossessed must first be promised and then quickly carried out. When it is not done, the people under threat of displacement may resort to agitation and the situation like Narmada agitation may be developed for the inhabitants of the upper reaches of the river across which, the building of a dam is planned. In case of substantial projects, a bread winner in each family can be employed in the project itself. The temporary shelters for the displaced persons should be built in a compact area so that their togetherness remains intact. Every care must be taken to meet the time frames of the project components and to guard against mis-management, inefficiency and corruption. Bureaucratic

delays and poor planning and control cause inflation of expenditure and losses to the public as well as the government. The projects involving land or forests should first be cleared by panchayats so that people have an opportunity to give their views before final approval. Every project has to be subjected to system analysis and besides this the total analysis will also involve value judgement whether the project could have an adverse effect on the cohesion and accord in the society.

For development to have roots in the soil, the education and training of the locals should be the first priority. The slogan of development in the Soviet Union was electrification. Rail and road communication, canal irrigation ushered prosperity in the Punjab. In NEI communications are perfunctory, in the current state of technology, NEI has to have air communication as its chosen mode. Helicopter stations should be constructed in cooperation with West Bengal and Bangladesh which will provide destinations for heli-borne trade particularly of perishable horticulture flowers and fruit and also give a boost to the tourist trade. Development will remain superficial unless most citizens are made literate and all children are provided schooling.

Education and Training

Primary education should be in the language spoken in the homes of the majority of children. After three years of education, primary school children may be started on learning elementary English and in high school elements of a language of choice between Bengali, Hindi or Assamese may be introduced in a short intensive course. All language courses must be tailored to give an introduction to science and technology. Since NEI is a late starter, there is all the more reason that the NEI children and adults have to exert in learning and practicing science and technology. There can be special workshops organized in school vacations for children to learn workshop practice, glass blowing,

photography, nursing and the handling of instruments for medical diagnosis. The institutions in India and private industry can assist in this effort.

Parents are to be convinced to send girls to school where they can learn the arts better which can help the family in their professional work if any dealing with land, domestic animals, forest produce and preparation of silk yarn or cloth. All India schemes for midday meals for children should apply in NEI. Most high schools should have farms or dairies or carpentry etc. workshop attached to them and any child able to work for an hour or so in these should be paid an hourly wage for his/her work. Many students after middle school should be offered seats in one year skill schooling and learn some professional skill needed to run a tailor's shop or laundry or a bakery etc.

The technical schools should run two-year courses for high school qualifieds to qualify for an engineering or electrical diploma. These schools should preferably be run by selected universities. A bright diploma holder can hope to get later after earning three years credit by part-time studies and university residence, a degree in Engineering or in applied science. Credits for a degree in applied fields will include subjects like welding, deciphering of X-ray photographs for hospitals, deciphering of satellite pictures of crops and forests, photogrammetry, analysis of seismic soundings for exploration, familiarity with rocks and crystalline structure etc. High science is very much involved for quicker development especially the new developments in molecular biology, advanced electronics, computer applications etc. For all this NEI has to produce soon its own experts so that they can attract outside experts to collaborate with them for the advancement of NEI.

The traditions that contribute to manners and human intercourse will continue. The society can develop only by education and intelligent experimentation. The education should not diminish but add to the pride in belonging to a clan and a tribe and the country. The child's primary religion

'Adi Dharma' should be respectfully explained to him/her. The tribal totems: animals or birds should command respect, and first works of art and pottery should naturally start with them. The tribal values are eternal values like love of nature, pride in achievement, physical fitness and truth. The Indian *Sanatan Dharma* was not anything different from the tribal *Adi Dharma.* The values of Secularism and Humanism are already there and have to be strengthened. The Meena tribals of Rajasthan have nothing to learn for speedy justice that does not harm the personality of the guilty. There are no crimes or unrepentant criminals in twenty-eight Meena communities who periodically conduct a Meena court for reforming the possible astray members. In modern days of democracy and human rights, the expulsion from the area of jurisdiction has to be replaced by social boycott which is as effective.

Position of Women

In NEI, traditionally women are treated as inferior to men. This has to go in the march to a developed society. This is necessary not because women are now loved more, but because the challenges before a developing society are such as can be met by the joint efforts of both men and women. When women get their equality, their contribution will surprise men. Particular emphasis is necessary on the literacy of women and the schooling of the girl child. Women should be entitled also to become *siems* or *myantries.* Literacy of women and schooling of girl children must be taken up on priority. Radio programmes where they reach the villages must be rich in useful instructions for girls and women in their family and society duties. Such programmes would include instructions regarding the crafts practiced by women in the households. First-aid and elements of nursing could be taught in schools. Women will easily excel in collecting and processing herbs for export as well as home use from their traditional knowledge. Women can be encouraged to

form cooperative societies engaged in trade, dairy and food products as is being energetically done by women in Maharashtra and Gujarat. Tagore was keen on this at Santiniketan. Art work of village women in Uttar Pradesh and Bihar has now a world market. Most of the work in dairy section all over the world is carried out by women.

Culture

NEI has to jump across from primitive tribal democracy to post-modern democracy in which all rules and laws are arrived at after broad discussion and an effort made to have them acceptable to all. NEI is lucky to escape the phase of feudalism and reach direct the environment of democracy and recognition of individual merit.

India has not yet seen the full participation of NEI in national and international sports. Sports must be made a national concern in NEI. They can have numerous teams performing in sports, dance and music and many national and international teams must have fixtures in NEI. The NEI troupes can be good ambassadors for NEI culture and aspirations. The ministry at Delhi could establish a library of short films on cultural events in NEI and in India as well as countries that come close to NEI in geography and terrain, e.g. countries of South East Asia and South America. The officials of the ministry when they visit NEI can introduce these films to audiences there. NEI must not take the apparent easy option of differentiated citizenship. India has already suffered enough from a caste system. The traditional authority of Siems, Bakhrawas and Langdoughs will naturally be clipped. But such honorary titles can be granted to new leadership and superior gifts as the Padma awards. There should be constituted a think tank in view of less developed daily and weekly etc. newspapers. This think tank should publish views regarding modifications in traditional practices and laws.

The chief officer in the district will look after the welfare of linguistic minorities. Descendents of immigrants in the past would be granted citizenship or rehabilitated with minimum discomfrot. Santhal minority should be treated as full citizens when they have contributed to the economy. Further parcelling of land as homelands is not in the interest of NEI. They should concentrate on more integration of people, more cooperation especially when land has to be managed when scattered in homesteads without the possibility of large scale farms. Cooperation in farming and trading activities will substitute for large scale farming.

More attention is to be given to the ancient trade in cinnamon bark and silk with south east China. India has to provide insurance cushion to Indian traders going east or north from NEI. Mexico has good experience of organizing cross border trade and would be happy to share their experience. NEI commerce with Bangladesh and Kolkata should have same support from India as they give to commerce of Nepal and Bhutan. Public discussions should be held on all subjects of interest to the population. This will substitute for shortcoming in media coverage. High degree of cooperation between leaders and public figures is conducive to healthy development. Ethnic struggles can be smoothed only by economic prosperity. Common culture will evolve by education and fellow feeling by conviction and easy communication.

Modernization cannot afford to neglect local preferences and these should receive priority in development and integration. We no longer can depend on the society of small independent villages or homesteads subsisting in their isolation and pride. NEI will benefit when people assemble and communicate. Feasts of merit should not be frowned upon but wastage can be avoided. Same holds for Moetze ceremonies. Characteristic Fairs of every locality should be encouraged and the occasion utilized for publicizing development efforts. National aversion to sexual licence and necromancy should be kept in view in public

displays. District officers would benefit from emulating Akbar's efforts in all directions of nation building. Guru Nanak was the first saint of India to speak against superstition masquerading as religion. Transmigration of souls and rebirth are also superstitions inspired by faith and have no scientific foundation. These are simply beliefs promoting contentment. NEI is in need of reconstruction from foundations avoiding entrenchment of unearned stature or inequality.

Humour and Charity

Programmes that spread humour and promote charity should be encouraged when collection drives are arranged for community projects. In the Punjab there is great vogue for arranging *Karseva, i.e.* free voluntary labour for projects like anti-mosquito spray, anti-pollution measures for springs and tanks, re-surfacing of village roads usually leading to the local gurdwara, temple or bus stand. NEI is well known for pithy sayings and proverbs, an education in themselves. There can be exposure of the public to these from various regions. Youth can organize drama clubs and raise travelling drama teams as is officially being done by the public relations departments of various states of India. *Kathas* and mythological stories if enacted will always pull crowds for entertainment and promotion of well-being. India is rich for market place shows of all kinds. A song fest is essential for any gathering.

Mineral Resources

Mineral resources are NEI's assets and minerals should be carefully extracted. Coal extraction in Kentucky (USA) impoverished the land and made it ugly, but the Canadians, when they extracted coal, converted the pits to sunken gardens which have become tourist attraction. NEI has some deposits of uranium, so much sought after by the nations of

the world for developing atomic energy. The reserves should be carefully estimated and guarded. For the present only such amount should be extracted per annum, as can be utilized in auxiliary industries based on radioactive materials. Economic potential and geological outcrops of the hills should be determined. Japanese style assembly of gadgets and instruments from components supplied by the electronic and optical industries should be attempted in small scale. Rural banking and entrepreneurial loans and insurance has to be in place for capable individuals at government's risk. A central photo-copying and knowledge distribution system without profit should be set in place which can utilize the expertise of documentation centres of the country and make the job more efficient for free distribution. Forestry and agriculture also require now high science and scientific education has to be encouraged as well as media activity.

Curbing Negative Elements

(a) ***Narcotics***: Development of Drugs and their distribution has to be under strict control. Illegal manufacture of drugs and their export is a great temptation for criminal syndicates. The rebels in any country are interested in narcotics trade and its profits being funneled to them. Such trade is an international crime. Recently certain eastern towns in NEI were considered to be centres of international trade in narcotics from production points in India and from the gangs in west Asia for distribution centres in Thailand and further east. Poppy cultivation which is not authorized for legitimate use in India, must be curbed including steps like destruction of standing popy crop.

(b) ***Rebellion as an Industry***: In certain countries suffering anarchy and dishonest government, rebellion is operated as an industry. They export terrorists and armaments to rebels elsewhere making enormous profits. Even big nations keep supplying arms and training to their

pet rebels and terrorists so long as their operations fit in the foreign policy of the big nation. Temptation for clandestine gun-running is quite high. NEI having soft borders with many countries has to be on guard regarding mischievous elements in the region. Another ploy of rebels and terrorists is to run an abduction and protection racket. As an example, the National Socialist Council of Nagaland possibly a splinter group of old rebels of Nagaland is demanding hefty protection sum in crores from the oil exploring ONGC of India before they begin their operations of discovering oil for future prosperity of the land when the state government is itself a co-partner of the ONGC for this venture and the corporation has the green signal from the state as well as the central governments. We hope the common people of Nagaland and NEI wake up soon from the danger to their development efforts and possibility of prosperity from the so-called revolutionaries who have criminal leanings.

7

Notes

Globalization

Globalization means lowering of trade barriers and as a corollary a free flow of capital and labour. At present many nations are directly or indirectly subsidizing production in certain sectors so that indigenous production can find purchasers in the market when imports are cheaper. Globalization desires elimination of such supports along with lowering of duties on imports. The multi-national companies are the chief beneficiaries of this globalization. The international banking tries to compensate the importing countries for their extra expenditure in arranging training of any displaced workforce for alternative remunerative work. The multi-nationals become the agents of transfer of know-how and of skills.

Real globalization will come when the exchange rates become logical based on price paid in local currency for the similar set of goods. The globalization will proceed as the prodution of the set of goods considered essential is distributed all over the world for levelling prices world-wide.

For quicker globalization the world can consider an easier exchange rate (dollars per unit national currency) for food items, Maslow needs, electronic aids for education, books and power needs and a floating rate for luxury items including armaments, aeroplanes, satellites, nuclear energy items, which enable countries to strive for more science and

technology. As the world evolves towards *mustopia* true globalization will also be reached.

Mustopia

Within the next couple of centuries, if global peace lasts, the world will become attuned to international collaboration, from the current attempts at globalization, and the activity of the democratically chosen and expanded security council. There will be further consolidation of international law and even proposals for universal civil code safeguarding the requirements of exceptionally situated groups. The aim would be of making the world a singly human family. The former utopias proposed by Plato and other philosophers and saints were usually aimed at few like minded people. Now the common desire would be for a *mustopia* or an unavoidable utopia covering one and all in the entire world. The coming world culture will be based on friendship and trust.

The strengthening of the UN governance and active interest and cooperative efforts of all nations and the rule of law will enable the world to progress with their national development projects good for them as well as for their neighbours. The time to achieve increasing prosperity, increasing welfare, educational and recreational activities is almost infinite like the billion years for which earth is likely to remain the playground of human beings. Sky is the limit of human achievements, prosperity and cultural activities for increasing leisure and healthy longevity. There will be lot of scope for constructive work and for learning new skills, or for travelling and pursuing favourite hobbies and teaching of children and less educated persons.

Immediate national and international programmes for reaching the high road to *Mustopia* like humanist economics, remunerative work for everyone softening of national borders and pursuit of science and technology have been detailed in the authors book *Human Eternity* published by

Concept Publishing Company, New Delhi in 2006. Continuous use of emerging technologies for conservation of soil, water, and environment for the whole world will be carried out.

New Mahayana

(See author's publication in 1997 on Foreign Policy)

Mahayna is the popular form of Buddhism that spread far and wide in the century before the birth of Christ and prevailed over the whole known world for few centuries. Besides the Buddhist teaching for the individual's advancement in the spiritual quest, the Mahayana included worship of many saviours (Bodhisattvas) and gods so that it became acceptable to many communities. What the international communal peace needs is tolerance and coexistence of all systems of thought. Similarly for international peace, coexistence of differnt political and economic systems can be tolerated. This in essence is New Mahayana. Any changes have to be brought about only through non-violence and democratic discussion.

New Mahayana is essentially secularism and humanism. It recognizes new values of multi-religious beliefs and the complexity of human mind.

Sarvodaya

Sarvodaya (Sanskrit) stands for development of everyone. Mahatma Gandhi used this term to emphasize that he was not for the development of any particular class like labour, farmers, dalits, or Brahmans or merchants but for development of all citizens irrespective of gender, caste or creed. He disagreed with the belief of communists in class war or the fanatics of every breed who cared only for their favourite groups. His politics was mixed with his piety and life strong faith in humanism of human beings. He found a

good person in every man or woman and had sympathy and best wishes for all.

Secularism

Most reformers hark back to the humanist roots of society. One with a secular outlook is repulsed by fanaticism of every kind of the right or the left. He is devoted to human welfare and security and expansion of human rights. To him society can be reformed and bettered only by democratic persuasion and never by violence. At about the time Guru Nanak was singing his message of love and brotherhood in the Punjab, George Fox was courageously spreading the humanist message in England.

Propagation of secular outlook will proceed hand in hand with the spread of the scientific approach. New symbols of cultural integration will evolve. In time secular prayer places will be attached to all temples, mosques and churches, or erected within the cherished monuments and heritage places in every multi-religious community. All religions constitute pillars of a multi-religious society, and deserve all respect and consideration. A secularist has faith in human wisdom to consider improvements in the functioning of all religions.

Bibliography

S.K. Agnihotri et al., (2005): *Perspective of Security Development in NEI,* Concept Publishing Company, New Delhi.

Senjit Baruah and P.W. Bank, (2005): *Durable Disorder, Contemporary Africa,* Oxford University Press, Van Nostrand, N.Y.

Maya Chaddha, (2000): *Building Democracy in South Asia,* Vishal Publication, New Delhi.

S.T. Das, *The Life of North East,* Gian Publication, New Delhi.

B. Datta Ray (ed.), (1983): *The Emergence of Middle Class,* Uppal Pubication, New Delhi.

Nan O'Day, (2004): *Dimensions of Terrorism,* Rock Aldgate Publication, New York.

Bimal J. Deb, (ed.) (2004): *Secularism and Conflict Resolution in NEI,* North East Council for Social Science.

Yu Guangyuang (ed.), *China's Socialist Modernization,* Foreign Press, Beijing.

Anil Kabuj, (2004): Complexity of Naga Peace Talks, *J. of Inst. Def. Studies and Analysis,* p. 694.

Biloris dyndem and U.K. De (eds.) Education in North East India (2004): Concept Publishing Company, New Delhi.

Emil E. Melizia, (1985): *Local Economic Development,* Pracyed Books, New York.

Mills (1973): *The Ao Nagas,* Oxford University Press.

Nanda, J.N. (1997): *Foreign Policy of Co-existence,* Ashish Verma Publication, New Delhi.

Nanda, J.N. (2006): *Human Eternity,* Concept Publishing Company, New Delhi.

Tifikit Nongbri, (2003): *Development of Ethnicity and Gender,* Rawat Pub., Jaipur.

Martin Ramstadt (2004): *Hinduism in Modern Indonesia,* Routledge Curzon, London.

Ramnika Gupta (ed.), *Aam Admi (Hindi),* Ramnika Foundation, Defence Colony, New Delhi.

Shin J. Yama Shita and J.S. Eades (eds.) (2003): Globalization in South East Asia, Pracyed Books, New York.

Gurnam Singh (ed.), *Ethno-nationalism and Emerging World Disorder,* Ind. Council of Soc. Sc., New Delhi.

Kartar Singh, *Rural Development,* Sage Publication, Ambala, Punjab.

Ed. staff, (India Today—Travel Place) (2006): *Travel in North East,* pp. 188, 200, 202.

Index